Explorations in Computer Science

SECOND EDITION

R. Mark Meyer

Canisius College

JONES AND BARTLETT PUBLISHERS

Sudbury, Massachusetts

BOSTON   TORONTO   LONDON   SINGAPORE

World Headquarters
Jones and Bartlett Publishers
40 Tall Pine Drive
Sudbury, MA 01776
978-443-5000
info@jbpub.com
www.jbpub.com

Jones and Bartlett Publishers
Canada
6339 Ormindale Way
Mississauga, ON L5V 1J2
CANADA

Jones and Bartlett Publishers
International
Barb House, Barb Mews
London W6 7PA
UK

Jones and Bartlett's books and products are available through most bookstores and online booksellers. To contact Jones and Bartlett Publishers directly, call 800-832-0034, fax 978-443-8000, or visit our website, www.jbpub.com.

Substantial discounts on bulk quantities of Jones and Bartlett's publications are available to corporations, professional associations, and other qualified organizations. For details and specific discount information, contact the special sales department at Jones and Bartlett via the above contact information or send an email to specialsales@jbpub.com.

Cover images © Photodisc

Library of Congress Cataloging-in-Publication Data

Meyer, R. Mark.
  Explorations in computer science / R. Mark Meyer.-- 2nd ed.
      p. cm.
  Includes index.
  ISBN-13: 978-0-7637-3832-7 (pbk.)
  ISBN-10: 0-7637-3832-8 (pbk.)
  1. Computer science. I. Title.
  QA76.M497 2006
  004—dc22

                              2005030302
                                 6048

ISBN-13: 978-0-7637-3832-7
ISBN-10: 0-7637-3832-8

Production Credits
Acquisitions Editor: Timothy Anderson
Production Director: Amy Rose
Marketing Manager: Andrea DeFronzo
Editorial Assistant: Kate Koch
Manufacturing Buyer: Therese Connell
Cover Design: Kristin E. Ohlin
Composition: Northeast Compositors
Printing and Binding: Courier Kendallville
Cover Printing: Courier Kendallville

Printed in the United States of America
15 14 13 12 11   10 9 8 7 6 5

Table of Contents

Preface

Welcome to *Explorations in Computer Science*. This lab manual accompanies the textbook *Computer Science Illuminated, 2/e* by Nell Dale and John Lewis, Jones and Bartlett Publishers, ©2004. The goal of this lab manual is to provide online, computer-based activities that will reinforce the concepts presented in the textbook.

The labs in this manual are arranged and numbered to follow the chapters of *Computer Science Illuminated, 2/e*, except for Lab 1, which introduces skills needed to work with this manual. In those cases where there is more than one lab for a given chapter in the textbook (for example, Labs 3a, 3b, and 3c), each lab focuses in-depth on a particular topic covered in the text. Teachers can assign all of the labs, or can pick and choose which ones to use in order to tailor the course to their needs and priorities.

Assumptions

Since *Computer Science Illuminated, 2/e* is targeted for CS-0 courses, the activities in this lab manual assume that students have the skills necessary for a course at this level. For instance, it is assumed that the students have no prior experience with programming, though they probably have basic skills with a computer. Therefore, this manual does not attempt to teach anyone how to turn on the computer, use a mouse, or drag a window. One of the essential skills that students may not yet have is how to take a picture of what is on their screen (often called a *screenshot*), and this is explained in the first lab.

Another assumption is that students using this lab manual are not taking the course solely to learn a particular programming language, but rather to be exposed to the wide variety of topics within the realm of Computer Science. This assumption mirrors that of the textbook. There are enough activities for students to get a good feeling for algorithms and programming, but these do not form the majority of the materials presented.

Since this lab manual refers to specific pages in the textbook, students should have their copies of *Computer Science Illuminated 2/e* with them as they work through the activities. Detailed explanations of the core topics, such as what job scheduling is and how it is used in an operating system, are not recapitulated in this manual. Rather, the students are referred to appropriate chapters and pages. The lab manual commences with an explanation of how to use the applet provided on the CD and how to interpret its behavior. In a few instances throughout the book, the author couldn't help interjecting some historical or other material deemed of interest.

Organization of the Labs

Each lab begins with succinct Objectives, References, and Background sections that briefly describe what is to be learned, what applets are to be used, and where in the textbook to find further information. Then the Activity section describes the software and shows how to use it. Students are expected to work through the Activity section, which guides them through starting the applet, comparing what they see on their screens to the screenshots in the lab manual, and completing the activities. This will prepare them to complete the Exercise sections. The teacher may assign one or more of the exercises to be handed in later.

The Deeper Investigation section provides a stimulating coda for advanced students. A further activity is briefly described or a question posed. In most cases, the appropriate response would be a one-page written answer to the question. In other cases, the teacher may assign the task posed by the Deeper Investigation.

Software

One very important goal of this manual is that students must be able to do the activities on any computer. In order to meet this goal, we include a CD with the lab manual, which has nearly all the software in the form of Java applets that can be run on any modern web browser.

The minimal software requirement for the lab is a web browser (Netscape 4 or higher, Internet Explorer 4 or higher, Linux Konquerer) with Java enabled.

All the applets were written using Java 1.2 and AWT graphical user interface components for maximum compatibility and widest audience availability. See the section below if you have trouble running the Java applets on your PC.

For one of the labs accompanying Chapter 12, we chose to use the spreadsheet program Microsoft Excel. Excel is a widely established program, available on both Windows and Macintosh. Students who use Microsoft Works instead will find no difference in the Works formulas, as least as far as the simple exercises that this lab manual poses are concerned. Linux and Unix users can use compatible products such as OpenOffice or SUN's StarOffice, which uses the same formulas and even read and write Excel files. In some cases, students may not have access to any of these programs and can either skip the exercise or adapt it to whatever spreadsheet program to which they do have access. (Alas, the Microsoft Access database program is not as universal as Microsoft Excel – in particular, there is no Macintosh version. This is why we chose to use an applet for relational databases.)

Getting Java to Work in Your Web Browser

The applets and applications in this lab manual are all written in Java. Consequently, you will need Java's run-time environment (JRE) to run them. You will need the version that we used in Java 1.2, so you may need a newer JRE.

Applets are java programs that run "inside" a web browser. That is, when you click on an html file or visit a web page that has a Java applet in it, the Java applet should start running automatically. If it doesn't, you will get a blank area where the applet would have been, and sometimes a message like "Applet not initiated."

Several years ago, court battles between Microsoft (makers of Windows XP and the Internet Explorer Browser) and Sun Microsystems (owner of Java) resulted in Java not being automatically included in Microsoft's popular web browser, Microsoft

Internet Explorer (MSIE). However, anybody can install Java on their Windows PC and run Java applets. It's just that you may need to do this step once after you get a new computer.

Here's how to get Java applets to run. First, go to Java's web site: www.java.com. When you reach that page, if you see a cartoon movie playing, then Java is installed and usable through your web browser already. (The movie changes every few months so describing it is pointless, though it is always humorous, colorful, and has some tinny music accompanying it.) You can also click on "Verify installation" on the left side of the page to make sure your browser can understand Java.

But if you need to install the Java JRE, click on the "Help" link for more information, which is immediately above "Verify installation." You can "Manually download" and install the JRE, too. There's a link on http://www.java.com.

The above steps are all you need to use this lab manual. More adventurous students may want to compile Java programs as well, in which case you need to download the development kit. Go to http://java.sun.com and click on J2SE download. (J2SE stands for Java version 2 Standard Edition, which is free.) You could choose either J2SE 5.0 or J2SE 1.4.2, although the Java code in this lab manual was tested using J2SE 1.4.2. Remember, this step is *not* necessary if you merely want to run existing applets and applications.

How to Run the Software

Students can run the software directly off the CD included with their lab manuals by selecting the lab they want from the index. Nine of the applets also exist as stand-alone Java applications. This allows students to run the software on their computers outside a web browser, enabling them to load and save data files. For security reasons, a Java applet that sits on a web page cannot load or save files, making it impossible for students to turn in their work in the form of electronic files. Therefore we use screenshots as a way for students to document their work on the applets. In some cases, the lab instructor might prefer that students run the software as a stand-alone application when available, and then save electronic files that they can turn in.

Remember that Java applets are quite universal and can be used on almost any platform: Windows (in all its versions), Macintoshes, Linux, Unix, and other systems. Java's graphics are also standard so applets that are written on one platform usually look identical, or nearly identical, on widely different platforms. This cuts down on development time and costs, and assures that the largest possible number of students can use the software. However, applets are, of course, somewhat limited in what they can do in order to foil viruses, worms, and Trojan horses.

Like most textbooks and all computer software, this lab manual and its accompanying software are evolving creations. Software problems and design issues have been addressed in this new edition and will be addressed in future revisions. Comments, suggestions, and field spottings of perhaps not-rare-enough bugs are definitely welcome. We hope students enjoy the exercises as they wind their way through this vast and fascinating landscape called Computer Science!

Acknowledgments

Numerous people have motivated this work and also made it possible. The kind folks at Jones & Bartlett Publishers set me on the path to writing this while we were visiting at SIGCSE '02 in Covington, Kentucky and discussing the new textbook *Computer Science Illuminated*. However, this conversation would not have happened but for Dr. Jeffrey McConnell, chair of the Computer Science Department at Canisius College, who steered me toward the Jones & Bartlett booth. I sincerely thank him for this nudge that set a vast machine in motion.

A huge debt of thanks goes to Kelly Bucheger, who wrote two of the labs and fixed others. He has taught the CS-0 lab at Canisius for over twelve years and is a popular teacher on campus. A saxophonist, composer, and writer on jazz by profession, he rounds out his days teaching Computer Science and web design at several area colleges, including Canisius College. While possessing all the other attributes of a great teacher, namely compassion, gentleness, clarity, and fairness, he brings an essential ingredient to the lab: humor. Kelly knows how to make the lab time fun while motivating learning. We all strive for this but he has accomplished it. Hopefully students across the country and the world who read this lab manual will feel this spirit of fun in their adventure into Computer Science!

R. Mark Meyer

Laboratory

Introduction to the Labs

Objective

....

■ Learn the skills you need to work with this lab manual.

References

....

Software needed:

1) A web browser (Internet Explorer or Netscape)

2) Applet from the CD-ROM:

   a) Introduction applet

3) (*Optional*) A word-processing program, such as Microsoft Word

4) (*Optional*) A spreadsheet program, such as Microsoft Excel or Microsoft Works Spreadsheet

Background

Everything you need to learn is explained in the Activity section below.

Activity

In these labs, you will sometimes be asked to take a screenshot of what appears on your computer screen. A screenshot is a "snapshot" of your computer's screen. This section discusses how to do this on a wide variety of computer systems.

In order to make them usable on as many platforms as possible, all of the applets in this lab manual were written using Java 1. While a later version of Java, version 1.4, allows printing directly from a Java program, many sites have not yet installed it, and it does not work with all browsers. That's why you'll need to rely on taking screenshots in order to record your work with the applets. Once you've taken a screenshot, it can be copied into a word-processing program and scaled, or it can be printed as is.

There is much variety in the way screenshots work on different platforms. For two platforms (Windows and Macintosh), the operating system offers a convenient way to take a picture of the screen. Other systems (Linux and Unix) require programs to take screenshots. Fortunately, these programs are widespread and free, so you should be able to take a screenshot without installing any software.

Most of the labs in this manual are designed to work universally on the vast majority of platforms without needing special instructions tied to a specific operating system. However, because each operating system has its own way of handling screenshots, specific instructions are given for the Windows, Macintosh, Linux, and Unix systems. You should jump to the section that covers your operating system, read the material, and then move on to the Exercise section for this lab.

Windows

Windows is a generic term that signifies a number of different operating systems from Microsoft. They include Windows 95, Windows 98, Windows ME, Windows NT, Windows 2000, and Windows XP.

In all versions of Windows, you can take a screenshot by pressing a button on the keyboard labeled *Print Screen*. It is often in the top row of the keyboard, to the right of the function keys. Sometimes the label *SysRq* is underneath *Print Screen*, signifying that taking a screenshot requires holding down the *Shift* key while pressing this key.

To take a screenshot, hold down the *Shift* key and press *Print Screen*. It will appear as though nothing happened, but the computer did make a picture of your entire screen and saved it in the system clipboard. To view this picture or print it out, start a program that edits pictures. Every Windows installation comes with Microsoft Paint, which works just fine for our purposes. Start Paint from the *Start* button on the task bar or create a new Paint document (often called a "bitmap image"). Then click on *Edit* in the menu bar and select *Paste*. The image will appear in your window, and Paint will resize the document to hold the entire image.

Macintosh

Macintosh refers to a line of computers manufactured by Apple Computer, including the imac, the ibook, the Powerbooks, and the G4 towers. These directions work on all flavors of Mac OS, from System 6 to MacOS X.

To take a screenshot on a Macintosh, hold down the *Shift* and *Apple* keys, and press *3* or *4*. *Shift-Apple-3* causes the whole screen to be "photographed," while *Shift-Apple-4* causes a set of crosshairs to appear, allowing you to select the part of the screen you want to appear in the image.

Once you've taken your screenshot, a new file appears on your hard drive with the name Picture1, Picture2, etc. To view the file, double-click on it, which usually brings up SimpleText, a bare-bones editing program. You can print your screenshot from SimpleText.

LINUX

Linux is the name of the Unix-like operating system created by Linus Torvalds in 1991. It has since gained a solid following and is used by a number of companies, schools, and individuals. Linux is most often encountered as a *distribution* under a particular name, including Red Hat, Mandrake, SUSE, Lycoris, Lindows, and others. These distributions contain the complete Linux operating system, system and programming tools, some applications, and other tools for configuring hard disks and installing software.

Almost every Linux distribution contains a program called **gimp**, which is an acronym for GNU Image Manipulation Program. (GNU is an acronym for a set of programming tools that predates Unix but that is now commonly distributed with Linux. GNU stands for GNU's Not Unix and is a recursive acronym, because on expansion the letters GNU endlessly repeat.)

Linux may start up in command line mode, rather than in graphical mode. You cannot use most web browsers in command line mode, except for Lynx (a very old, text-only browser). If your Linux computer is in command line mode, start X Windows to go into graphical mode. Typically, you would type the command

```
$ startx
```
(the dollar sign is the prompt, not part of the command).

To take a screenshot with gimp, first start gimp. Either find its executable and double-click on it, or type the command `gimp` from a shell. These directions apply to Version 1.2.1 and higher. You can get gimp free from *http://www.gimp.org*.

Gimp will create several small windows. The main one has many buttons on it and a title of "The Gimp." Pull down the *File* menu and select *Acquire*. Then select *Screenshot* from the submenu. You can either take a screenshot of one window or of the whole screen. You can also set a delay, such as five seconds, so that you can put the image you want on the screen by starting the desired program. Once gimp takes the screenshot, it brings up a viewing window. To save the picture, click once inside the image itself to bring up a new menu. Select *File* and *Save As*.

UNIX

Unix refers to a large number of operating systems descended from AT&T's original Unix, including BSD, System V, Solaris, Irix, AUX, AIX, and many, many others.

To use a web browser in Unix (other than the text-oriented Lynx mentioned earlier), you need to start a windowing system. Some vendors such as Sun have their own (SunView), but most also run X Windows. The details of starting the graphical user interface vary, so you should consult your lab instructor.

Once you have a screen you want to take a picture of, start up a program that will take a screenshot. Sometimes these are called snapshots. Look for an *Acquire* menu. Some programs to try are xview and xpaint.

If you are running X Windows on a Unix computer, gimp (the GNU Image Manipulation Program) will work. Gimp was written for the X Windows environment in Unix and was later ported to Linux. You can download it for free and either install it or have the local system administrator install it. Check out gimp's web page at *http://www.gimp.org.*

For details about X Windows and its desktop environments, go to *http://www.rahul.net/kenton/xsites.html.*

Exercise 1

Name _____ Date _____

Section _____

1) Start the "Introduction" applet (from the CD-Rom). This simple applet contains some fields for you to fill in, including *Name*, *Major*, etc. There's also a pull-down menu from which to choose your class (*Freshman*, *Sophomore*, etc.).

2) Fill in the fields with the appropriate information.

3) Once you've finished filling in the information, take a screenshot of the completed applet.

4) (*Optional*) Paste the screenshot into a word-processing document. For example, if you're using Microsoft Word in Windows, your screenshot is stored on your machine's clipboard after you take it, so you can simply launch Word and paste the image into the Word document. If you are using Word on a Mac, take your screenshot, launch Word, go to the *Insert* menu, and choose *Picture From File...* Browse your way to the picture and select it.

Most word processors that can handle images will let you re-size them, permitting you to put several screenshots on a single page. This will be handy for future labs that require multiple screenshots. Consult your program's Help section or check with your lab instructor for instructions if you wish to do this.

5) Print your screenshot.

Deliverables

Turn in your printed screenshot.

Laboratory

Exploring Number Systems

2

Objectives

- Experiment with number systems.
- Gain practice adding in binary and converting between bases.

References

Software needed:

1) A web browser (Internet Explorer or Netscape)

2) Applets from the CD-ROM:

   a) Number systems

   b) Binary addition

Textbook reference: Chapter 2, pp. 32–51

Background

Everything you need to learn is explained in Chapter 2, "Binary Values and Number Systems."

Activity

Part 1

First review positional notation of numbers in several bases, including decimal (base 10), binary (base 2), octal (base 8), and hexadecimal (base 16). See pp. 35–40 of your textbook.

Then bring up the "Number systems" applet and experiment with converting a few numbers, both from decimal to the other base, and from the other base to decimal. For example, try this:

Type the decimal number 26 into the top text area, and press the *Convert* button next to it (or simply press *Return* after you type the decimal number). You will see 11010, which is 26 expressed in binary.

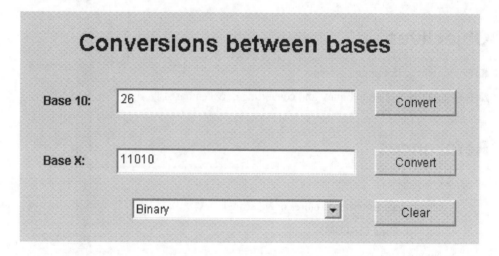

Now try converting in the other direction. Type 7777 into the *Base X* text area. Now, before you press the *Convert* button, you need to tell the applet what base 7777 is a numeral of. Could it be binary? Base 5, even base 7? (If you're not sure, read p. 38 of your textbook.)

7777 could be decimal, octal, or hexadecimal. Pull down the choice bar and select *Octal*. Now you can press *Convert*!

What did you get? 4095? Try verifying that the applet didn't make a mistake (always a smart thing to do, considering that applets are software, and software is written by people, and people make mistakes).

$$
\begin{array}{rcl}
7 \times 8^0 = 7 \times 1 & = & 7 \\
7 \times 8^1 = 7 \times 8 & = & 56 \\
7 \times 8^2 = 7 \times 64 & = & 448 \\
7 \times 8^3 = 7 \times 512 & = & \underline{3584} \\
& & 4095
\end{array}
$$

Some calculator programs, such as the Windows Calculator, also allow you to convert between decimal, binary, octal, and hexadecimal.

Part 2

Now you will hone a skill crucial to a budding computer scientist, which is binary addition. While it might seem unfamiliar at first, binary addition works much the same as addition in the decimal system you know and love, where adding numbers in a column will sometimes generate a carry value that must be added to the column to the left.

First review binary addition on pp. 39–40 of your textbook. Make sure you understand the process of generating a carry from one column to the next left one. Here's a handy review table:

$$
\begin{array}{cccc}
{}^{0}0 & {}^{0}0 & {}^{0}1 & {}^{1}1 \\
+0 & +1 & +0 & +1 \\
\hline
0 & 1 & 1 & 0
\end{array}
$$

The smaller number to the left and above the bigger numbers is, of course, the carry. It must be added to the next column to the left, unless it is in the last column, in which case it just drops down.

One thing that textbooks seldom show is a table where the carry-in is added to the two digits, producing the sum bit and the carry-out. The reason is probably due to space constraints, since two digits and a carry-in would give eight combinations. However, we can quickly cut that down to four combinations, because four of the possible combinations are the same as previously shown, when the carry-in is 0. So here's the useful part of the three-bit addition table:

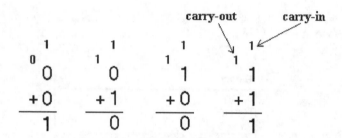

Using this table, see if you can do the binary addition shown on p. 39 of the textbook yourself. Remember that if there is no bit, just pretend there is a 0.

Now start the "Binary addition" applet. Type 5 into the top box on the far right, labeled *Decimal*. Type 7 into the box below it. We want to start off with easy numbers so we can verify the applet ourselves.

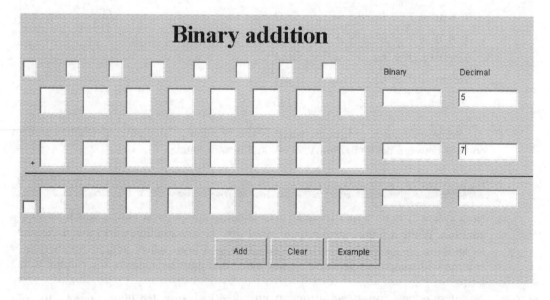

Now press the *Add* button and watch it go. First, the applet converts 5 to binary, which is 101, and stashes that in the top binary box. Then it converts 7 to binary (111) and tucks that into the bottom box. Next, it splits those binary numbers into bits and pads them on the left side with 0s. (Why do you suppose computers insist on putting "useless" 0s on the left side of numbers?) Finally, the applet animates its addition, column by column.

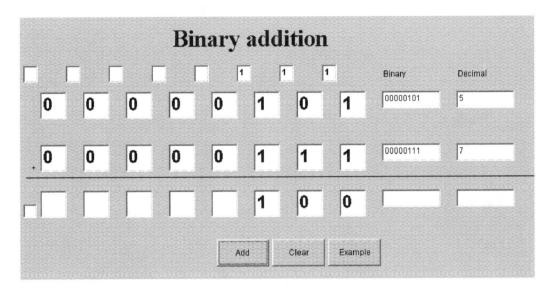

When it is done, you will see 00001100 both in the *Binary* box and split up into bits. Can you convert that into decimal? You can confirm on the applet screen that it's 12.

Many of the applets in this lab manual have an *Example* button (or buttons) that you should explore. The *Example* button usually displays a harder task than you might think of inputting yourself. In later labs, the examples show you complex patterns that would take too long to type in. In any case, press it now to see what the applet does.

Deeper Investigation

Many anthropologists believe that most human societies use base 10 (decimal) for their counting system because we have ten fingers. (Why people don't use their toes as well, hence favoring a base 20 system, is a good question. Perhaps during the Ice Ages people had to keep coverings on their feet when they tramped from continent to continent!)

There are a few interesting discrepancies. For example, the ancient Babylonians had a base 60 system, which shows itself still today in our minutes and seconds, and in our 360-degree compasses.

Imagine what kinds of problems you would have to solve if you insisted on using a base 60 system. What would your calculator keypad look like? Would it be practical?

An even deeper question is what base 1 would look like. Base 2, 3, 4, 5,...8,...10,...16, and even 60 are all very similar. In base X, there are X symbols, from 0 up to (X-1). These symbols are multiplied by powers of X. But what about base 1? If you multiply 1 by any power, you still get 1. However, base 1, also called *unary*, actually has a place in theoretical computer science. Describe what a base 1 number would look like and how you could convert between decimal and unary.

Laboratory

Representing Numbers

3A

Objective

■ Learn how negative numbers and real numbers are encoded inside computers.

References

Software needed:

1) A web browser (Internet Explorer or Netscape)

2) Applets from the CD-ROM:

   a) Negative binary numbers

   b) Real number representations

Textbook reference: Chapter 3, pp. 52–66

Background

Everything you need to learn is explained in Chapter 3, "Data Representation."

Activity

Part 1

There are a number of ways to encode negative numbers in binary. Two common methods are sign-magnitude representation and two's complement representation, explained in your textbook.

To begin, start the "Negative binary numbers" applet. In the top text area, type a negative number, such as −67. Either press *Return* or click on the *Convert* button, and you should see the following:

Negative Number Representations

Your decimal number:	-67 Convert to Signed Binary
Number of digits in binary	8
Sign-magnitude form:	11000011
2's complement form:	10111101

Every representation needs to know the number of digits in the binary number, and that is set in the second text area. Eight is a common number of digits (we should be proper and call these binary digits *bits*), because a byte contains eight bits and the byte is widely used today as the smallest unit of addressable memory. (The analogy between bits and bytes and eating was too irresistible for early computer scientists, who noticed that a four-bit unit was also quite useful, especially in early coding schemes such as BCD (Binary Coded Decimal). What do you suppose they called the four-bit unit? Elementary, my dear computer science student! A *nibble*, since it is half a byte.)

The sign bit is highlighted in gray in the two bottom text areas. Try typing in a positive number and look at the forms. What sign bit do you see?

Part 2

Real numbers are, well, real important to computer applications. Early computer scientists had a hard enough time figuring out the best way to represent integers. But the need for real numbers arose from the hard sciences—physics, chemistry, engineering. Computer manufacturers invented a number of ways to encode the vital pieces of a real number for science and even business. Sometimes these representation methods were incompatible with other computers. CDC (Control Data Corporation) was one of these maverick manufacturers.

Eventually, an international standard IEEE 754 was agreed upon, and has been used in all chips since. (IEEE is the Institute of Electrical and Electronics Engineers and 754 is the number of the document defining the standard.) You can be rest assured that your computer's central processor chip uses IEEE 754 encoding.

To begin, start the "Real number representations" applet and type in some numbers with fractional parts, such as 2.5 and -373.4698. Press *Return* or click on the *Format* button. This applet re-formats the decimal real number three ways: in scientific notation (see textbook pp. 65–66), as a decimal fraction multiplied by a power of 2, and as a binary fraction.

Let's study the number 2.5. First, 2.5 is already between 0 and 10, so we merely multiply it by 10^0 (which is 1) in order to get it into scientific notation. Next, we note that the applet said $2.5 = 0.625 \times 2^2$. Since 2^2 is 4, 4 x 0.625 is 2.5. Most real number representations (including IEEE 754) place the decimal point in the leftmost position and make sure there is a 0 to the left of it. This contrasts with scientific notation, which specifies that the digit left of the decimal point must be larger than 0 but smaller than 10.

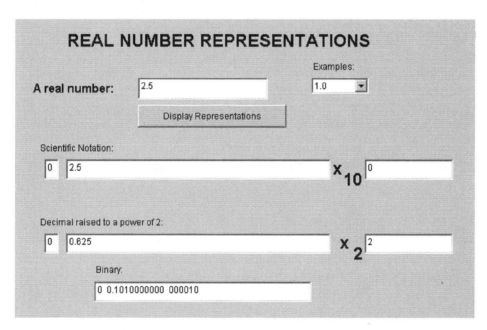

Finally, let's look at the binary representation at the bottom of the screen. 0.101 is not a decimal number but a binary one. Positional representation, which was reviewed in Chapter 2 of the textbook (p. 35), can be extended so that digits (or bits) to the right of the decimal point are multiplied by appropriate powers of 2. The first place after the 1's position (which is 20) is the halves position, or 2^{-1}. Since 2^{-1} is 0.5, we call this spot the halves place. The second place to the right of the point is the fourths place, or 2^{-2}, which is 0.25. But since there is a 0 in that place in 0.101, we do not add 0.25 to our ongoing sum. Finally, the eighths place has a 1 in it, so we add 0.125, which is $1 \div 8$, or one-eighth.

$$0 \cdot 1 \quad 0 \quad 1 \quad 0 \quad 0$$
$$2^0 \quad 2^{-1} \quad 2^{-2} \quad 2^{-3} \quad 2^{-4} \quad 2^{-5}$$

Adding 0.5 and 0.125, we get 0.625, which is our mantissa. Multiply that by 2^2, which is 4, and we get 2.5, our original number.

Notice that a 1 appears in the two smaller text areas to the left of the numbers if the original number is negative. Real numbers use signed-magnitude representation for the overall number.

Exercise 1

Name _____ Date _____

Section _____

1) Start the "Negative binary numbers" applet.

2) Type in −1 and press *Return*. Study the result. Find the sign bit. How does the applet indicate it?

3) Change the number of bits to 32 in the text field "Number of digits in binary" and convert −1 again. Write down how the two forms of binary −1 are different in 32 bits compared to 8 bits. (Feel free to convert −1 into 8 bits again to see the different forms.)

4) Make a small table as follows:

	4	−4
8 bits		
12 bits		
16 bits		
32 bits		

5) Fill in the binary values for these two numbers, changing the number of bits from 8 to 12, then to 16, and then to 32.

6) Without using the applet, guess what −1 and −4 would look like using 64 bits. Write down your guess.

7) Change the number size back to 16 bits. Type in 32767 and press *Return*. Describe what you see below.

8) Now type in -32767 and convert. Write down the values. What is the difference between $+32767$ and -32767 in 2's complement form?

9) Type 4 into "number of digits in binary." Then convert the number 8. What do you see? Does this seem right?

Exercise 2

Name _____　Date _____

Section _____

1) Start the "Real number representations" applet.

2) Type in a fairly large number, like 9419876302, and press *Return*. Write down the value in scientific notation and in binary.

3) Experiment with a few other numbers. What generalization can you make about the powers of 10 and 2 that you see? (Hint: Which power is bigger? Is it always bigger by the same amount? Try dividing the bigger by the smaller. Is this ratio always the same or close to the same?)

4) How many bits does the binary representation at the bottom of the screen devote to the mantissa (the part after the binary point and separated by a space from the binary power)?

   What would be the smallest mantissa that could be represented? (Hint: You may need a calculator.)

5) Type a number such as 0.00000000123 and press *Return*. What is the sign of the exponent?

6) Type several other numbers in and press *Return*, noting the binary representation at the bottom of the screen. What observation can you make about the first bit to the right of the binary point?

7) Fill in the following table by typing each number into the top text field and pressing the "Display Representations" button.

0.5	
0.25	
0.125	

What do you notice about the mantissa (the string of bits after the point)?

What happens to the exponent?

What would the next number in the table be? (Hint: each number is 1/2 the number above it.)

Deliverables

Turn in your hand-written sheets showing your answers to the exercises.

Deeper Investigation

Computers love binary because of the bistable devices out of which we build them (discussed in Chapter 4 of your textbook, pp. 96–101). These devices have only two stable states, ideal for representing 0 and 1 but nothing else. But the fact that we like to see numbers in decimal and computers work in binary leads to some problems, similar to the impossibility of representing $1/3$ exactly as a decimal fraction.

In the "Real numbers representations" applet, type in 0.333 and press *Return*. Write down what you see in the scientific notation area. Then type in 0.3333 and repeat. Are you surprised? Why do you suppose the applet prints out this weird value?

Now type in 0.1 (one-tenth) and press *Return*, looking at the binary representation at the bottom of the screen. It is a bit deceptive to look at what the applet puts out. Try to come up with some combination of the negative powers of 2 that *exactly* equals 0.1. Can you do it? What does that mean about a computer representing 0.1? (You mean a computer can't even represent ten cents?!?!?!)

Because of these inaccuracies in number representations, called *roundoff errors*, early computers that were destined for business used a different method of representing dollars and cents, a method that would not be subject to roundoff errors. It was called the *packed decimal* method. See if you can find out more about the packed decimal. (One good reference is the *Encyclopedia of Computer Science*, Anthony Ralston et al., editors, Nature Publishing Group, ©2000.)

Failing that, figure out how one could use integers to represent dollar amounts exactly. What kinds of problems would still arise? (Hint: Think about interest rates!)

3B

Colorful Characters

Objective

∙∙

- Learn how colors and text are represented.

References

∙∙

Software needed:

1) A web browser (Internet Explorer or Netscape)

2) Applets from the CD-ROM:

   a) Character codes

   b) Text translator into ASCII

   c) Color maker

Textbook reference: Chapter 3, pp. 66–82

Background

· ·

Everything you need to learn is explained in Chapter 3, "Data Representation."

Activity

· ·

Part 1

As you've learned, every kind of data in a computer must be represented by a sequence of ones and zeros. Computer scientists and engineers had to be enormously clever in representing the myriad data forms using only 1s and 0s: text, numbers, sounds, colors, still pictures, moving pictures, smells, . . . Wait! Smells? No, not yet (perhaps never!).

Now that we know how numbers of all kinds are represented using 1s and 0s, the next step is to learn how characters are represented. A character *mapping* assigns a number to each character, and then this assigned number is encoded in binary. For example, a very simple mapping scheme might assign 1 to A, 2 to B, and so on. A computer would then store B as 10, the binary representation of 2. It is as simple as that—except for making everyone agree on which mapping to use!

Pitched battles have been fought over character mappings. Well, that is a bit of an exaggeration, but it did take a long time for the computer industry to stop using many different mappings. IBM mainframes used EBCDIC while CDC (Control Data Corporation) supercomputers used their own system. DEC (Digital Equipment Corporation) and other smaller companies used ASCII. Perhaps the big breakthrough came when the IBM PC was announced in 1981. Though it was an IBM, it used ASCII and ever since ASCII has grown until it is practically the only character mapping used nowadays.

Except for Unicode, that is. With the advent of Java and web browsers and the growing international community of computer users, the Unicode character mapping has enabled us to encode virtually every written symbol as a 16-bit number. Not all software uses Unicode, and not every PC or computer can support Tibetan or Chinese script. But the mapping is in place, supported by international standards organizations. To learn more about Unicode, go to *http://www.unicode.org*.

The "Character codes" applet provides a way to type in a number, using either decimal or hexadecimal, and see the corresponding character. Following is a screenshot:

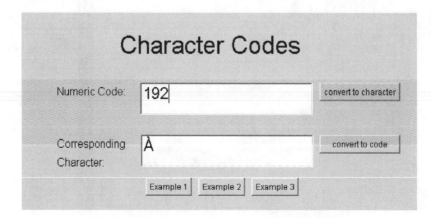

After typing in 192 in the numeric code text area, press *Return* and you will see À, which is A with a grave accent. You could also have typed `0xC0`, which is the hexadecimal number for 192. (The `0x` in front is a C-like way of designating that the following number is base 16, or hexadecimal. `x` is an abbreviation for hexadecimal.)

Try the example buttons. Example 3 cycles through all characters from 33 up to 255. If your computer can't represent a certain character, Java substitutes a little square.

Part 2

The "Text translator into ASCII" applet makes it easy to type in some text and have the computer translate all of it to binary using the ASCII character mapping.

Start the applet. Notice the character mapping in the tall text area on the left. It starts at 32, which just happens to be the blank character, and ends at 127. The codes that are mapped into the numbers 0 through 31 and 127 on up are unprintable. They have names and some are used in various functions, but in general they do not produce any graphical image on the screen.

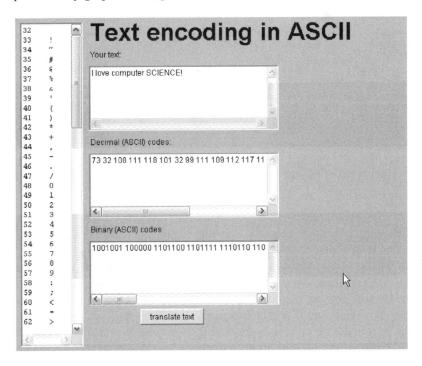

Inside the computer's memory, there are no spaces between the seven-bit chunks that represent each character. The computer just "knows" how wide a character is and counts off bits accordingly.

Most computers today store one ASCII character in a byte, which is eight bits, not seven. The ASCII character set was extended to include 128 extra characters, many of them for PC graphics. Then Unicode came along and re-defined it all again. But the 128 codes with numeric values from 0 to 127 have remained stable.

Your textbook gives all 128 ASCII characters on p. 64. This is a two-dimensional table, unlike the one-dimensional table in the applet. For example, to find the code for "z," put together 12 and 2, which results in 122.

One of the characters, number 8, is called BEL. Can you guess what it does? (It sounds a beep on the computer.) Many of the others were used in early telecommunications equipment. For example, STX is "Start of text" and ACK is "Acknowledge."

Part 3

The "Color maker" applet shows you two ways that colors can be encoded using 1s and 0s. The first method is called RGB because it represents colors as combinations of three intensity values of the colors red, green, and blue. The second method is called HSB, because it represents colors as combinations of three values on the scales of hue, saturation, and brightness. RGB is discussed in detail on pp. 77–78 in your textbook.

To begin, start the "Color maker" applet, and select *Red* from the color name choice pull-down menu in the bottom left corner. The applet sets the scrollbars and text areas to the values according to the RGB encoding and the HSB encoding.

Feel free to play with the sliders and select other colors. Notice how the colors change in the bar near the bottom of the screen. The name of the color choice in the menu does not change, however, when you change the color above by means of the sliders or by typing values into the text areas.

RGB represents the red, green, and blue values as integers from 0 to 255. Since 255 is the largest number that can be represented in eight bits, it follows that RGB requires 24 bits (8+8+8) for one given color. No wonder they call it 24-bit color! Since 2^{24} is 16,777,216, there are nearly 17 million different colors that can be represented in 24 bits. There is nothing magical about using eight bits except that it matches the size of a byte, the fundamental unit of computer memory in most machines nowadays.

HSB represents the hue, saturation, and brightness as real numbers between 0 and 1.0. Leave the saturation and brightness values at 1.0 and slide the hue value up and down. Notice how the color goes from red to yellow to green to blue to magenta. The saturation number determines how much white is mixed in, and the brightness determines how strong the intensity is. If it is low, then it is like seeing the color in very dim light or a dark room.

Compare the colors *red* and *pink* by pulling down each name choice and looking at the values. In HSB, the hue value stays the same, but the saturation goes from 1.0 to about 0.31. However, the RGB version of pink shows that mixing in more green and blue with a lot of red creates pink, too. Neither RGB nor HSB is the "correct" way of viewing colors; they are just alternate ways. However, most computers store colors in RGB and convert to HSB when needed.

In summary, there are many different ways of encoding the same information in 1s and 0s. There are many different character mappings, several different ways of storing colors, and multiple ways of representing audio (see textbook p. 74).

Exercise 1

Name _____ Date _____

Section _____

1) Start the "Character codes" applet.

2) Type 75 into the top text area and press *Return* (or click on the *Convert to Character* button). Write down what you see.

3) Type in 107 and do the same. What relation does this character have to the first one?

4) Do the same for 76 and 108, and for 77 and 109. Write down the codes and the characters you see.

5) What conclusion can you draw about how upper- and lowercase characters in ASCII are represented, based on your experiments?

6) If you were writing a function to capitalize text for a word-processing program, what simple transformation would you make to the character codes to capitalize a letter?

7) Now type in 200, 201, 202, and 203, one at a time, writing down what you see.

8) What characteristics do these characters share?

9) What does ASCII code 199 look like? What language uses this character?

Exercise 2

Name _____ Date _____

Section _____

1) Start the "Text translator into ASCII" applet.

2) Type in a short sentence or phrase.

3) Press *Return* or click on the *translate* button.

4) Take a screenshot.

5) Suppose that you wrote an essay and your word processor reported that it contained 10,000 characters. How many bits would your computer need to store the essay using ASCII codes? How many bytes is that?

6) Scroll the tall window at the left to see all the ASCII codes. Write down the numerical codes for these symbols:

_____ $\frac{1}{2}$

_____ $\frac{1}{4}$

_____ $\frac{3}{4}$

_____ $\times$ (multiplication)

_____ $\div$ (division)

_____ $\pm$

Exercise 3

Name _____ Date _____

Section _____

    1) Start the "Color maker" applet.

    2) Select *Green* from the names choice pull-down menu. Write down the RGB and HSB values.

    3) Now select *Magenta* and do the same.

    4) Using more common color names, what color is magenta?

    5) Suppose you heard that Kathy's favorite color was 0,255,0. What would Kathy call that color?

    6) Pick a color from the pull-down list of names in the center, and gradually slide the saturation scrollbar toward the top so that the value in the box below "Sat" goes down to 0. What color do you end up with? Is this true of any color?

7) Pick another color from the pull-down list and gradually slide the brightness scrollbar toward 0. What color do you end up with? Is this true of any color?

8) Page 78 of your textbook gives several color names that are not in the pull-down list. Let's see what *maroon* looks like. Type 140 into the Red box and press return. Then type 0 into the green box and press return and do the same for the blue box. Take a screenshot of the applet. (You may not have a color printer. If not, take a black and white screenshot anyway and ask your professor to use imagination when grading.)

Deliverables

Turn in your hand-written sheets showing your answers to the exercises. Also turn in one screenshot for the "Text translator into ASCII" applet and another screenshot for the "Color maker" applet.

Deeper Investigation

The CDC character set started with A = 1, B = 2, C = 3, and so forth. If you were creating a character mapping, this is probably what you would do. However, the CDC character set didn't have lowercase letters like a, b, or c. (The original character set used six bits and so there weren't enough possible number combinations.)

ASCII and EBCDIC do not use A=1, or even a=1. However, there are regularities in the character coding scheme. You discovered one such regularity in the previous exercises. Are there any others in ASCII that you can find?

Try to find a listing of EBCDIC's codes, most likely on the Web. You will find some surprises. For example, A=193, B=194, C=195, . . . and I=201. But J=209. What?!?!? There are no similar breaks in ASCII. There was a reason for the breaks in EBCDIC, but you may have to dig to find out what it is. (Hint: if you get stuck, punch the keys of your computer, but not too hard!)

Switching to a different train of thought, think about how arbitrary encodings tend to be. Suppose we wanted to encode the four primary directions of the compass. Would we choose North=1, South=2, East=3, and West=4? Are there any particular reasons for choosing other mappings? (Hint: Think about telling a robot to turn completely around, smoothly, without changing directions.) Also, have we shown ethnocentrism by setting North to 1? (Have you ever seen a map of the world where the South Pole is at the top? Australian restaurants love to pin these on the wall to test the sobriety of their customers.)

Write down your views on why computer scientists veer away from completely arbitrary encodings, based on all that you have learned in this lab.

Compressing Text

Objective

- Learn how text can be compressed.

References

Software needed:

1) A web browser (Internet Explorer or Netscape).

2) Applets from the CD-ROM:

   a) Text compression using key words

   b) Text compression using Huffman encoding

   Textbook reference: Chapter 3, pp. 69–74

Background

Everything you need to learn is explained in Chapter 3, "Data Representation."

Activity

Part 1

These days when computers have lots of megabytes of RAM and vast gigabytes of disk space, you might wonder why text compression would be so important. In a word: *networking*! Today's computers are almost always networked, sending and receiving text, pictures, video, and sounds. That's a lot of data, and unfortunately the data pipes that all this stuff must go through tend to be narrow (metaphorically speaking). Lots of people are still struggling with 56 Kbps modems at home, and even T3 lines at big universities can't keep up with the demand for data. Obviously, the more we can compress data, the more data we can get through the overburdened networks!

There are many different ways of compressing a stream of 1s and 0s. Your textbook describes several of them, including run-length encoding, in which a sequence of identical characters can be replaced by a count of them. IBM used to store text files like this because there were long sequences of blanks in such files that need not be stored explicitly. Remember that a single blank is ASCII 32, so it requires eight bits like every other character.

Another method is key word encoding (textbook pp. 69–71). Start the "Text compression using key words" applet and click on the *example* button:

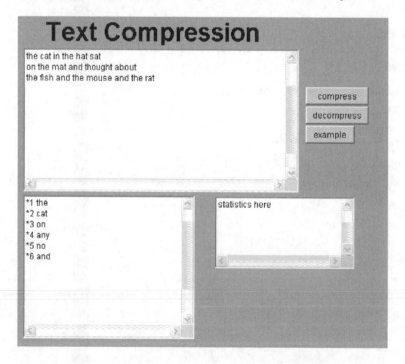

As you can see, the key words are listed in a table to the left, under the main text area. Each key word is identified by an asterisk followed by a number.

Click the *compress* button. The main text area is replaced with a compressed version of the text, in which the key words were replaced by their numerical codes. Decompressing should restore the text to its original poetical luster.

Notice that we only saved 8% of the total number of bits by compressing. That's not very much! Of course, our key word table is pretty small and incomplete. If we populated it with more words, we would expect the savings to go up.

Another consideration with key word encoding is that short words do not save much in compression, but long ones do. Choices have to be made, however—since it is unlikely that the word *antidisestablishmentarianism* will appear often in the newspaper or in web pages, assigning it an integer code is probably not useful.

In fact, the words *on* and *no* turn into *3 and *5, respectively, so we haven't saved any space at all. Furthermore, as we add many thousands of words to our list, the numbers themselves get rather long. It wouldn't make sense to replace *food* with *327839.

One last remark about key word encoding reveals some deeper questions about information. An old joke tells of a visitor to a comedians' convention. The visitor was surprised to see the comedians in the hall laugh uproariously as a comic onstage called out numbers: "417! 502! 29!" He finally asked the person sitting next to him what was going on.

"Well, you know," said the comedian, "we've been doing these conventions for so long that we all know the jokes by heart. To save time, we've assigned them numbers, and we just go by those."

"Well hey, even *I* can do this," thought the visitor. So he stood up and shouted "57!"

Stares and dead silence.

"I don't get it," he said to the man next to him. "Why didn't anybody laugh?"

"Sheesh," replied the comic, rolling his eyes. "Some guys just can't tell a joke."

The real joke is that without the table, explaining what the numbers mean is impossible.

Part 2

Another way to compress text is to use a variable length code, such as Huffman encoding. The key word encoding we used previously was variable length if the numbers were represented by ASCII letters, but if the numbers were stored as 32-bit integers, then it would not be variable length.

Huffman encoding is not one single mapping of letters to bit patterns. There are programs that generate the code table according to a frequency chart. Such programs are rather complicated and do not concern us here. We merely trust that they exist and can be used to create the code table.

For example, page 73 of your textbook gives a short code table that is suitable for some English words that only use the letters A, E, L, O, R, B, and D, and not having any spaces. DOORBELL is an example.

Start the "Text compression using Huffman encoding" applet and click on the *example* button. This puts DOORBELL into the text area and sets up the code table as given in the book. Click on *compress* and *decompress* to watch it work. How much room does it save?

Now click on *example 2*. This puts a longer message into the text area and sets up a table with all 26 capital letters, plus the blank. Click *compress* and *decompress* to watch it work. Notice how much it saves in space.

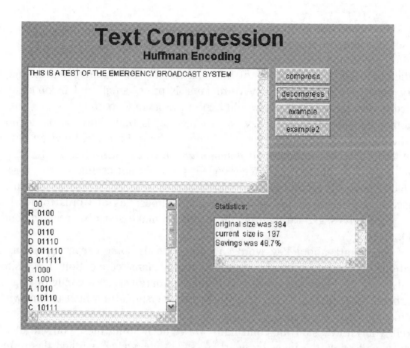

Huffman encoding is used quite frequently. The popular WinZip utility that compresses Windows files uses it. Such applications get even greater savings by creating a customized coding table for each document. First, the program counts the letters and makes a frequency table. Then it forms the Huffman coding table. Remember that the most frequently used letters are assigned the shortest codes. This coding table is stored along with the compressed document and must be read in before decompressing.

Exercise 1

Name _____   Date _____

Section _____

1) Start the "Text compression using keywords" applet.

2) Click the example button. Add more codes to the keyword table in the lower left corner so that the text in the top text field turns completely into asterisks followed by numbers when you click *compress*. Take a screenshot.

3) Could this compression method be used for encryption as well? (Encryption is when you scramble the message so that hostile eavesdroppers cannot make sense of it.) State why you believe it could or couldn't be used for encryption.

4) Enter a word preceded by an asterisk into the text area and press *compress*. What does the applet do? Does it decompress this correctly?

5) What would happen if you really needed to have the sequence *3 in your text? How would you modify the applet so it wouldn't get confused? (Hint: Choose another numbered code, like *99, and let that represent *5.)

Exercise 2

Name _____ Date _____

Section _____

1) Start the "Text compression using Huffman" encoding applet.

2) Click on *example 2* and *compress*.

3) Remove the first bit from the beginning of the encoded message and click *decompress*. What happens?

4) Take a screenshot.

5) What generalization can you make about Huffman encoding versus run-length or keyword encoding? How resilient are these methods to errors, which would probably arise as the bits flow through a network?

6) Clear the text area and type in XXXXXXXX, and click *compress*.

7) What happens to the space savings? Are you surprised?

8) The sequence of 1s and 0s used to represent a particular letter in a Huffman code is not arbitrary or random. Your textbook on p. 73 hints at the way a sequence is chosen. Given this, what can you say about the letter J? What about the letter E?

Deliverables

Turn in your hand-written sheets showing your answers to the previous exercises. Also turn in one screenshot for the "Text compression using key words" applet and another screenshot for the "Text compression using Huffman encoding" applet.

Deeper Investigation

Now is a great time to discuss one of the classic questions of computer science. There seems to be a trade-off between time and space, between computing effort (measured in seconds) and memory requirements (measured in memory cells). A program that goes to extra effort to produce the very smallest compressed file takes longer to run than a program that uses a pre-assigned coding table.

Here is the classic question: Are time and space always *inversely proportional*? (This means when one goes up, the other goes down.) In other words, as you save on time do you use more space? But if you spend more time computing, can you use less space? This trade-off is seen in many areas of computer science, but nobody can prove that it is truly necessary. (This "time versus space" question is really at the heart of the question as to whether Algorithm Class P is the same as Algorithm Class NP, discussed in Chapter 17 of your textbook, pp. 557–558.)

Think of some aspects of daily life in which you must consider trade-offs. It doesn't have to be time versus space, but it can be. For example, consider the following trade-off that comes to mind: The most difficult and time-consuming degrees yield the best-paying jobs. Do you agree?

Laboratory

Logic Circuits

4

Objectives

■ Experiment with digital logic circuits using a simple logic gate simulator.

References

Software needed:

1) A web browser (Internet Explorer or Netscape)

2) Applet from the lab website:

   a) LogicGates applet

Textbook reference: Chapter 4, pp. 96–112.

Background

Everything you need to learn is explained in Chapter 4, "Gates and Circuits."

Activity

Digital logic circuits are the bedrock of computer design. CPU chips such as the Intel Pentium or AMD Athlon are silicon wafers in which millions of circuits are embedded. Everything your computer does depends upon them.

In this lab, we will learn how to use the "LogicGates" applet to draw and test digital logic circuits. Chip manufacturers, such as Intel and AMD, use sophisticated (and extremely expensive) software to help them design and test their chips. But the basic idea is the same.

First, start the "LogicGates" applet. You can load a number of examples by pulling down the example choice pull-down menu. Load Example 1 "simple," as shown here:

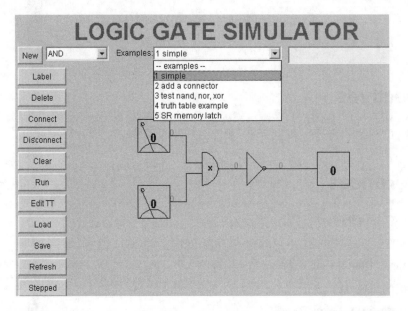

Each logic gate has a distinctive shape (see pp. 96–100). The wire coming out of the gate shows its current value. Gates are oriented so that their inputs come in from the left side and their outputs go out from the right side. This cannot be changed nor can the gates be rotated in this applet.

Two special boxes exist for input and output. The switch box has a lever in it along with 1 or 0. To flip the lever and change the value, click on the number right in the center. The other box has only 1 or 0 in it. This is the output box that accepts a wire from a gate and displays its value.

To propagate new values through the circuit, click on the *Run* button. It changes to say *Stop* so that when you click on it again, the simulator stops running. When the circuit is running, you can click on the switches and watch values change throughout the circuit.

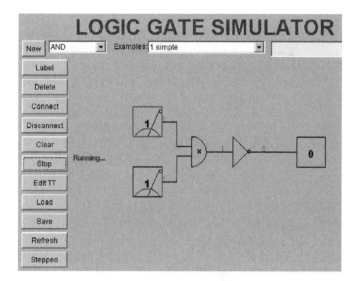

To practice using the simulator, we'll build the logic circuit shown on p. 105 of the textbook. First, if your simple example circuit is still running, press the Stop button. Now, clear the screen by clicking on the *Clear* button. To build the circuit, you'll need three switches, two AND gates, one OR gate, and one output box. To create them, click on the *New* button, pull down the gate menu and select the gate or other item you want. Then click once where you want the switch, gate, or output box to sit. You can reposition gates, switches, and outputs by dragging them to a new location.

Notice that when you are adding gates, the *New* button changes to say **New*. Most of the buttons in this applet work like this: they show they are still active by displaying an asterisk in front of the label on the button. Because the button stays active, you can click on different gates without having to re-click the *New* button over and over.

Click on the *New* button again to stop adding components. The asterisk will go away.

Let's also attach labels to the boxes to mimic the circuit diagram on p. 105. However, in the Logic Gate simulator, labels attach to boxes, not wires as they do in the textbook.

First click on the *Label* button, which allows us to label gates and switches. Then click on the top switch. A textfield opens up right above the switch. Type "A" into it and press Return.

Here's what you should see:

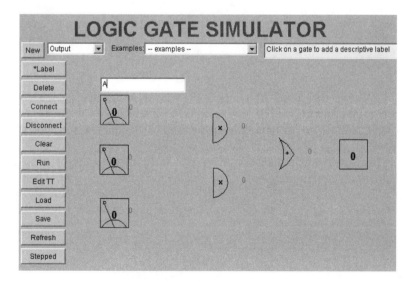

Label the middle switch as B and the bottom switch as C. Also label the output X. If you want to be complete, label the top AND gate as D and the bottom AND gate as E. When done labeling, click on the *Label* button so that the asterisk doesn't appear.

Now it's time to connect the gates, so click on the *Connect* button. Click once on switch "A." A red line flashes into view, anchored in the center of the switch and following the mouse pointer around the screen. Click on the top AND gate. Repeat this process and connect all the boxes so they match the screenshot below. If you make a mistake, click on the *Disconnect* button, then click on a gate. All lines between that gate and all other components will be removed.

A gate's output may have any number of wires coming out of it so that it connects to more than one other gate. Merely select the same gate as the left end of a wire more than once.

Automatic elbows break lines up into horizontal and vertical segments. To see a version that uses diagonal lines, click on the *Stepped* button. However, in most circuit fabrication technologies, all wires must lie on a grid so diagonal wires are either impossible or expensive. To see the elbowed lines again, click on the bottom button, which has changed from *Stepped* to *Diagonal*.

Sometimes the elbows make it hard to see overlapped wires, and that plagues this circuit. So move the bottom AND gate a little to the left until the wires show more clearly.

Here's the final picture:

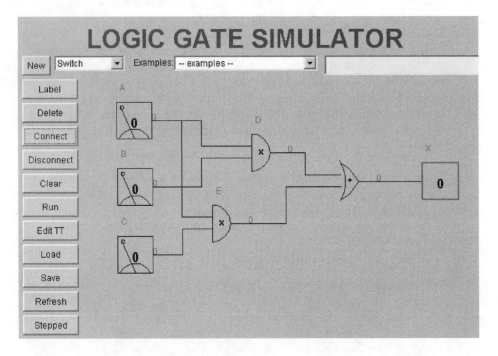

Now run the circuit by clicking the *Run* button. Click on the switches to change their values. Record the results in a truth table and see if the circuit gives you the same results as shown on p. 106 of your textbook. They had better agree! (They will, don't worry.)

Imagine what a terrible thing it would be if a major chip manufacturer's simulation software didn't give the right values and they sent a chip into production with flaws in it. Well, actually, don't bother imagining: It's already happened! In the early 1990s, Intel recalled their new Pentium processor when scientists and engineers pointed out that in certain calculations the chip gave the wrong answer! Analysts have estimated that this bug in the chip's division algorithm cost the company about $500 million. (Too bad they weren't using our simulator to check their circuit design!)

Our simulator provides you with six types of gates: AND, OR, NOT, NAND, NOR, and XOR. All of these are defined in Chapter 4 of the textbook. Another type of "gate" available in our circuit simulation is the *Truth table*, which allows you to avoid building really complicated circuits with lots of gates. Instead, you fill in the truth table values and the simulator treats it as a gate. A truth table "gate" can have two, three, or more inputs.

Let's build a circuit using truth tables. Clear the screen and add three new switches and one output.

The trickiest part is putting the right size truth table into the circuit. To do this, make sure the *New* button is activated (has an asterisk next to *New*.) Then pull down on the gates menu and bring *Truthtable* into view. In the yellow message box, Logic Gates will ask you how many inputs your truth table should have. The default is 2, but since we have 3 switches, replace the 2 with 3. Then click once in the middle of the area to create the truth table. Click off the New button and connect these gates as shown below:

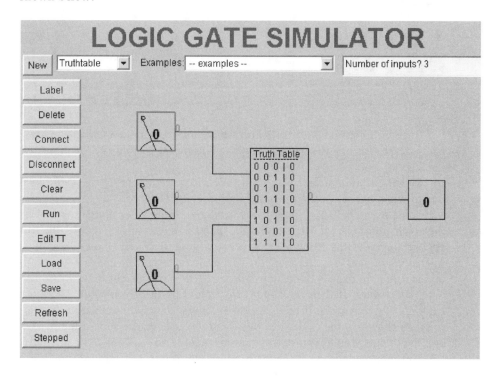

Important note! Make sure that when you connect the switches, you connect the top one first, then the middle one, and finally the bottom one. This is necessary because the order of the incoming wires determines which value is associated with which column in the truth table. The first wire connected will correspond to the first column in the table, the second wire will correspond to the second column, and so on. If you connect them in a different order, the wires going into the truth table will not correspond to the columns of your truth table.

New truth tables list all the input values in canonical order, but since the output is shown as always 0, we need to edit the truth table so it implements our desired output. To edit a truth table, click once on it (after making sure that all the buttons on the left are off, i.e., do not have asterisks in front of their names). This makes the truth table the top gate and its border will turn red. Now click on *EditTT*. A green window pops up, allowing you to edit this truth table.

The input values are separated from the output value by a vertical bar symbol (|). Go through the truth table and change some of the output values, as shown in the picture below.

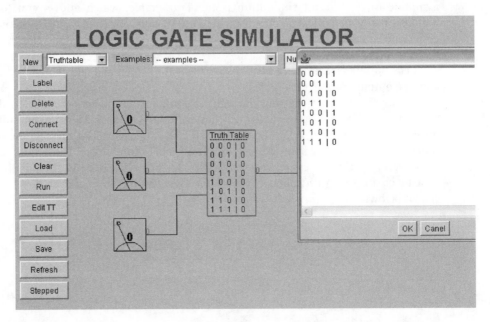

Once you are done, click OK to dismiss the truth table editing window, and then click on *Refresh* or just drag the truth table around so that the simulator will repaint the screen.

Run the simulator and play with the switches, comparing the value in the output box to what you see in the truth table. Do they match?

Since the truth table "gate" bypasses digital logic gates altogether and implements the given truth table, it might seem like using it is cheating! Actually, the truth table is similar to SSI chips, shown on p. 113 of your textbook. Sometimes we are more interested in the function that the circuit computes (the pairing up of inputs and outputs) than in exactly which gates are needed to implement that function.

By the way, if there are only two inputs to the truth table, there will be two columns and four rows. If there are three inputs, there will be three columns and eight rows, as shown in the example. Four inputs would require four columns and 16 rows, and five inputs would require five columns and 32 rows. Do you see a pattern?

The input values in all the truth tables you see in this lab are shown in canonical (standard) order, just like the textbook uses. This isn't necessary for the simulator to work properly, but canonical order helps us fallible, distracted humans keep track of our inputs and outputs.

Tip

LogicGates can be used as a standalone Java application. If you use it as an application (not an applet), you can load and save your programs. To run, navigate to the folder containing the LogicGates class files and double click on the **run_application.bat** file.

Exercise 1

Name _____ Date _____

Section _____

1) Start the "LogicGates" applet.

2) Add two switches, one XOR and one output, and connect them.

3) Press the *Run* button and try out all four combinations of inputs for the switches, recording the results in a truth table. Take screenshots for each combination.

Exercise 2

Name _____ Date _____

Section _____

1) Start the "LogicGates" applet.

2) Create the same circuit as previously, but this time insert a NOT box between XOR and the output.

3) Press the *Run* button and try out all four values by changing the switch values. You do not have to take screenshots, but again record the results in a truth table so you can see the values.

4) What does this circuit do? Study your truth table to determine its function. (Hint: It yields a true result only when inputs A and B share a particular relationship. What is that relationship?)

Exercise 3

Name _____ Date _____

Section _____

1) Start the "LogicGates" applet.

2) Build a new circuit that will be a larger version of the one you created in Exercise 2. There will be four switches. Assign them the labels A1, A0, B1, and B0. (Note: A1 is a way of specifying A_1 when you can't really have a subscript.)

3) The circuit will have two XORs, two NOTs, an output, and a mystery box, arranged as shown below:

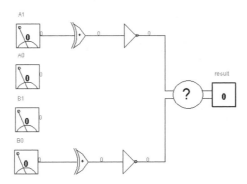

4) The purpose of this circuit is to compare two 2-bit binary numbers to see if they are the same number. For example, suppose A (that is, the two-digit number comprised of A_1A_0) is 10 and B (the two-digit number B_1B_0) is 10, then the output box will display 1. If A is 10 but B is 11, the output box will show 0, which is Boolean-ese for "false."

5) Connect the XOR boxes to the proper input switches. (Just think about how you compare two numbers for equality. What digits do you compare?)

6) The "mystery gate" is either AND or OR. You can either experiment until you get the right answer, or, better for your brain (and more impressive to your teacher) you can reason out which it should be.

7) Take a screenshot showing your circuit getting the correct result.

Exercise 4

Name _____ Date _____

Section _____

1) Start the "LogicGates" applet.

2) Build a circuit with three switches, two truth tables, and two outputs. Example 4 from the pull-down examples sets up some of this. Choose example 4 and add to it.

3) Set up one of the truth table boxes to implement the Sum column on p. 110 of your textbook, and the other to implement the Carry-out column.

4) Take a screenshot of your program after you run it on one of the combinations of the three inputs.

Exercise 5

Name _____   Date _____

Section _____

1) Start the "LogicGates" applet and build the following circuit. It has 2 switches, one output, and three NAND gates.

2) The wiring between the switches and the NAND gates is a little unusual. For both switches, connect the switch to the NAND gate adjacent to it *twice*. This will cause both the wires coming out of the switch to the same NAND gate, though the simulator will spread them out visually. (To do this, click on the *Connect* button, then click once on the top switch, then the top left NAND. Repeat this: click once again on the top switch and then on the top left NAND.)

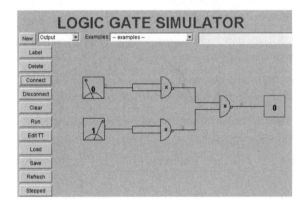

3) Experiment with the circuit by running it (click on the *Run* button) and change the switch values. Write down the 4 possible inputs and the output you see below:

Top switch	Bottom switch	Output
0	0	_____
0	1	_____
_____	_____	_____
_____	_____	_____

4) What logic gate has the same output?

5) EXTRA CREDIT: Replace the three NAND gates with NOR gates and run the circuit. What logic gate has the same output? Hint: it won't be the same as the answer to number 4.

Exercise 6

Name _____ Date _____

Section _____

A lot of students just do not believe DeMorgan's Law (p. 107 of your textbook) so let's see if the LogicGates simulator can prove it.

1) Start the "LogicGates" applet.

2) Add 2 switches and arrange them vertically on the left side of the panel. The top one we'll call A and the bottom one will be B.

3) We will implement both (AB)' and (A' OR B') in the same circuit. Add two outputs. One output will have the value of (AB)' and the other will have the value of (A' OR B'). If the output boxes read the same for all inputs, then we know that (AB)' = (A' OR B').

4) Since (AB)' is just the NAND gate, add one NAND gate and connect both A and B to it. Then connect the NAND gate to the top output.

5) For the (A' OR B') part, we'll need two NOT gates, connected to A and B. The output of these NOT gates goes into an OR gate, which then goes into the bottom output.

6) Run through all four combinations of binary values of A and B, writing down the two outputs. Are they the same? Is DeMorgan's Law true?

A	B	Top Output	Bottom Output
0	0	_____	_____
0	1	_____	_____
_____	_____	_____	_____
_____	_____	_____	_____

Exercise 7

Name _____ Date _____

Section _____

In this exercise we will create a simple multiplexer. Pages 110-111 of your textbook describe how a multiplexer selects which input signal will be copied to the output, based on a set of control lines. If we have 8 incoming signals, we need three select control lines, as shown in the book. Four incoming signals need only 2 select control lines, whereas 2 incoming signals would require only 1. (If you had 16 incoming signals, how many select control lines would you need?)

1) Start the "LogicGates" applet. In this circuit, we will create a multiplexor with two inputs and one control wire.

2) Put three switches in the panel and one output. Label one of the switches S0 and the other two D0 and D1. The S0 switch should be at the left edge and the D0 at the top, similar to the placement on p. 111. You'll need an output at the right edge, as shown below.

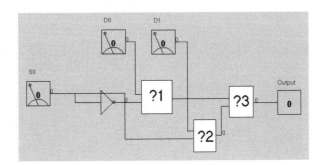

3) The tricky part is deciding what the logic gates inside the three mystery boxes should be. All three question mark gates are either AND or OR. You could experiment until you get it right, but let's apply a little brainpower.

The value in D0, whether it is a 0 or a 1, should be copied to the output box when the select control wire has 0 in it. Similarly, the value of D1 must be copied to the output box when S0 has the value 1 in it. This is why S0 is called a select control input, because it *selects* which of the two Ds gets copied.

Our task is to figure out which value of S0 will permit D0 through. However, let's tackle the easier case of figuring out which value of S1 will permit D1 through, and then we'll work backward from there.

When S0 is 1, we want D1. If we *AND* S1 and D1, then the output will be whatever D1 is, whether it is 0 or 1. But if S0 is 0, then we want D0 and not D1. So our AND gate will ignore D1's value and always give us 0.

By reversing our logic, we see that when S0 is 0 we want D0, so what operation do we apply to them? We can't quite use the same one as above (*AND*) because S0 being 0 would always give us 0. That is why we have to stick a NOT gate in there. Then S0' becomes 1 and if we AND that with D0, we get whatever D0's value is. (Remember that is either 0 or 1. The whole point is to *copy* D0's value through, not force it to be 0 or 1.)

Now we have two cases and two sets of gates: when S0 is 0, select D0's value. When S0 is 1, select D1's value. But we want just one output, not two!

What gate would take 2 or more wires, and "combine" their logic values? You won't get the answer directly here, so think hard about it. If both inputs are 0, the output should be 0. When either input is 1, the output should be 1. Hmmm....

4) Real multiplexors often select between 8, 16, 32, or even more inputs. As your book shows, the binary number represented by the values on $S_2S_1S_0$ permit one of eight data values to flow through to the final F output. Although our logic gate simulator is a little too primitive to permit large diagrams, you might try building one with 4 data inputs and two select control wires. You just might be able to squeeze it all in.

Deeper Investigation

The "LogicGates" applet can create some very complicated circuits. Its main limitation is due to the finite amount of space available—if you have very many gates, you'll eventually run out of room. However, judicious use of the truth table box can cut down on screen clutter.

Example 5 of the sample circuits in the applet is a model of the S-R latch shown on p. 106 of your textbook. It is called memory latch. Try running it. When it starts, the output boxes will cycle between 0 and 1. To stop that, click on one of the switches so that it reads 1. Now the circuit is stable. Experiment with it by setting one of the inputs to 1, then changing it back to 0, and watch the outputs change.

S-R latches are 1-bit memories built out of logic gates. Real computer chips use something like them in the main CPU for registers and other small, high-speed storage. Because the S-R latch has some serious timing problems, variants of it such as the clocked D-latch are used instead, as are even more complicated circuits called *flip-flops*.

S-R latches are circuits that have a peculiar characteristic about their wiring. Can you tell what it is? If not, pretend that the top switch pours a blue-colored liquid through the wires and the bottom switch pours a red-colored liquid. Trace the liquids with colored pens. What do you notice? What would you call this characteristic of S-R latch circuits? Your teacher might be able to give you a hint.

Because of this characteristic, circuits like the S-R latch are called *sequential circuits*. The output of sequential circuits depends not just on the current inputs, but also on the previous values on all the wires. They give a different *sequence* of results over time. Straight-through circuits like the one on p. 105 of your textbook are called *combinational circuits* because their outputs depend only on the combination of their input values.

Try to find out more about logic circuits. Look in some hardware books for an example of a flip-flop circuit. Try tracing its workings.

Laboratory

Computer Cycling

5

Objective

- Learn about the fetch-execute cycle of computers.

References

Software needed:

1) A web browser (Internet Explorer or Netscape)

2) Applet from the CD-ROM:

   a) Super Simple CPU

Textbook reference: Chapter 5, pp. 132–141

Background

Everything you need to learn is explained in Chapter 5, "Computing Components."

Activity

Computers are unbelievably complex, but at the lowest level they are surprisingly simple. A program consists of thousands, millions, or billions of instructions, all performed blindingly fast. But each individual instruction is quite simple.

If each instruction is simple and easy to understand, why does putting thousands of them together result in software that would tax the intelligence of Albert Einstein? People have been trying to figure that out for years, because figuring it out might give us clues to understanding, writing, and maintaining that software. The difficulty seems to be in what some call the *semantic gap* between problems that computer scientists want to solve using computers and the tools with which they solve them—tools meaning software, programming languages, and even hardware. If the tools are too simple, we will have to use a lot of them in complex ways to get the job done. If the tools are more complex, they can do more in one step and are easier to describe. Think of how much work goes into preparing a meal, but how easy it is to place an order at a restaurant. In this lab, we will study the instructions of a very simple computer and then watch programs run in this computer.

Start the "Super simple CPU" applet. Compare its components to the block diagram in Fig. 5.2 on p. 132 of your textbook. The input and output devices are merely text areas to the left. The CPU and memory are clearly marked, though the memory of this computer is ridiculously small: 16 words of memory, each 16 bits long, a total of about .0000305 megabytes!

Pull down to Example 5 to load the example program, and then click the *Run* button. After a few seconds, you should see this:

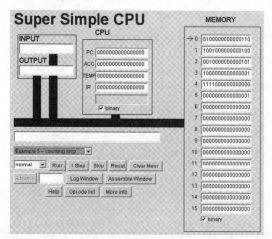

As the program runs, it cycles through the basic instruction cycle, which is commonly called the fetch-execute cycle (see textbook pp. 132–133). This applet displays the steps in the cycle in the blue text area in the middle.

There are three registers in this CPU:

PC   The program counter
ACC   The accumulator
IR   The instruction register

The PC register contains the address of the next instruction. It goes up by 1 after most instructions, but some, such as the JMP instruction, simply rewrite it entirely.

ACC is the accumulator, kind of like the one-number screen on many calculators. Values are added into it or subtracted from it, if the instruction is ADD or SUB. It also serves as the way station for values coming in from the input device and going out to the output device.

IR is the place where the current instruction is kept and decoded. In the applet, the decoded values from the current instruction are displayed below IR. The *mnemonic* of the instruction, a short alphabetic name for the instruction, is shown along with the operand in decimal.

The contents of memory and the CPU's registers are usually displayed in binary, but they can be shown in decimal by unchecking the box. This does not affect the values and can be done any number of times, even when a program is running.

Numbers are stored as 16-bit values in 2's complement notation (see p. 62 of your textbook). If the number has a 1 in the leftmost bit, it will be thought of as negative.

There is online help built into this applet. Click on the *Help* button near the bottom of the screen to bring up a window explaining the basic operation of the applet. There are also buttons that summarize the opcodes and give more detailed explanations of them.

OPCODES

Binary	Mnemonic	Short Explanation
1111	STP	Stop the computer
0001	ADD	Add accumulator to operand
0010	SUB	Subtract operand from accumulator
0011	LOD	Load memory cell into accumulator
0100	LDI	Load immediate into accumulator
0101	STO	Store accumulator memory cell
0110	INP	Input value and store accumulator
0111	OUT	Output value from accumulator
1000	JMP	Jump to instruction
1001	JNG	Jump to instruction if accumulator < 0
1010	JZR	Jump to instruction if accumulator = 0

MORE ABOUT THE INSTRUCTIONS

1111 STP	This stops the computer; no more fetch/decode/execute cycles until you reset.
0001 ADD	Fetch a number from memory and add it to the contents of the accumulator, replacing the value in the accumulator. (E.g., 0001000000001111: Get the value at memory location 15 and add that to the accumulator.)
0010 SUB	Fetch a number from memory and subtract it from the contents of the accumulator, replacing the value in the accumulator.
0011 LOD	Fetch a number from memory and store it in the accumulator, replacing the accumlator's old value. (E.g., 0011000000001111: Get the value at memory location 15 and store that value in the accumulator.)
0100 LDI	Load immediate; the value to be put in the accumulator is the operand (the rightmost 12 bits of the instruction); do not go to memory like LOD. (E.g., 0100000000001111: Store the value 15 in the accumulator.)
0101 STO	Store the accumulator's value in memory at the indicated location. (E.g., 0101000000001111: Store the accumulator's value in memory location 15.)
0110 INP	Ask the user for one number and store that in the accumulator.
0111 OUT	Copy the value in the accumulator to the output area.
1000 JMP	Jump to the instruction at the indicated memory address. (E.g., 1000000000001111: Put the value 15 into the PC, which will cause the next instruction to be taken from location 15 of the memory.)
1001 JNG	Jump to the instruction at the indicated memory location if the accumulator's value is negative; otherwise just add 1 to the PC. (E.g., 1001000000001111: Put the value 15 into the PC, if accumulator < 0; otherwise go to the next instruction.)
1010 JZR	Jump to the instruction at the indicated memory location if the accumulator's value is zero; otherwise just add 1 to the PC. (E.g., 1010000000001111: Put the value 15 into the PC, if accumulator = 0; otherwise go to the next instruction.)

Each instruction in this super-simple computer has two parts: opcode and operand.

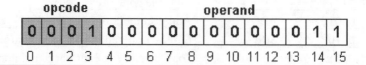

The opcode is the first four bits and represents the instructions. For example, 0001 is the ADD instruction, as the opcode reference list above shows. The operand can be several different things depending upon which opcode you are using. It is often the address of a memory cell, used by ADD, SUB, LOD, and STO. If the instruction is LDI (*load immediate*), the operand is a 12-bit constant that is put directly into the accumulator. The jumping instructions (JMP, JNG, JZR) use the 12-bit operand as the value that is stored in the PC register, thus causing control to jump to that spot in memory. A few instructions (STP, IN, OUT) ignore the operand altogether.

This CPU applet allows you to watch each instruction in almost microscopic detail. If the applet is running, press the *Stop* and *Reset* buttons. Then pull down the speed choice from the menu next to *Run* and select *manual*.

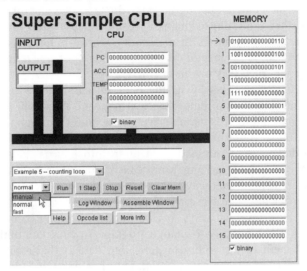

This allows you to control the steps of each and every instruction. Click on *Run* to start the program. Each instruction begins and does one part of the fetch-execute cycle before stopping. When it stops, the word "ready..." appears in the box next to the *Advance* button. Information on what is about to happen is provided in the blue box above the buttons.

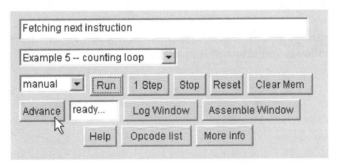

Using the *Advance* button to walk through instructions takes some time, but it allows you to carefully observe each part of each instruction. In addition, addresses and values that flow between the CPU and memory, and between the Input/Output unit and the CPU, are animated in yellow binary numbers through the red bus.

The normal speed disables the *Advance* button but still animates the instructions, while the fast speed does not show the animations, allowing the program to run quickly.

In addition to advancing each instruction, you can *single-step* a program. Single-stepping means to run one complete instruction and then stop the program by clicking on the *1 Step* button. Many debuggers for real programming languages also have a single-stepping option so you can dig into a problematic program and ferret out its bugs. Think of single-stepping as a sort of time microscope: You amplify the delay time between instructions to a very large amount so you can see what is going on.

There are a number of example programs, ranging from ridiculously short and simple to somewhat complicated. The greatest common divisor is fairly complex to understand, and it almost fills up the entire 16-word memory.

Load the GCD program (Example 6). Memory cells 0 through 10, inclusive, contain the program. Memory cell 14 contains the first integer value (in the example it is 18, which is 10010_2) and cell 15 contains the second integer (in the example it is 24, which is 11000_2).

It is extremely difficult to determine exactly what the program does by just looking at the contents of the memory. In fact, it is impossible to tell from memory alone whether a location contains a 16-bit integer or an instruction. So how does a computer "know" what is in a memory word? It never really does; only the PC determines that. If the memory word's contents are fetched into the IR and treated like an instruction, then they *are* an instruction.

Wait a minute! This opens the door to a terrible problem! What if a program "jumps" into a section of data? Can that happen? What will be the result? The answer to the second question is certainly *yes*, a computer can jump into data. This is one of the major implications of the *stored program concept* (textbook p. 132).

One downside of this ability to jump into data is that an improperly designed program can get the wrong jump instruction (because an improperly designed programmer wrote it that way!), start interpreting data as instructions, and probably do something terrible, like erase all of the memory or launch nuclear missiles. Hardware designers have invented ways to assure that this won't happen. Sadly, mean-spirited people can use this ability to change programs to write evil things called viruses.

One benefit of the ability to jump into data is that a program can create a new program, or even rewrite part of itself, and then execute it right away. Since programs are really data, this capability was seen by some early pioneers as a way programs could learn and improve. It hasn't quite worked out that simply because learning is a hugely complex process (as you well know!) but the spirit of this dynamic execution is used in many aspects of computer science today.

The purpose of the "Super simple CPU" applet is not to turn you into a programmer. But it is meant to allow you to see the fetch-execute cycle wend its path through a typical CPU. In the exercises, you will study a few instructions individually. The larger programs were included so that you can get a feel for how a complete program looks and acts at this low level.

Exercise 1

Name _____   Date _____

Section _____

1) Start the "Super simple CPU" applet.

2) Select the first example by pulling down the examples list and selecting "Example 1–sequence."

3) The program is three instructions long, in memory addresses 0, 1, and 2. Write down the three instructions or take a screenshot.

4) Click on the *Opcodes list* or *More info* button to get a key to the opcodes.

5) Decode the three instructions. Look at the first four bits of each memory cell and find those bit patterns in the opcodes key. Write down the corresponding three-letter mnemonic.

6) How many fetch-execute cycles will this program perform when you run it?

Exercise 2

Name _____   Date _____

Section _____

1) Start the "Super simple CPU" applet.

2) Load and run the second example, which contains an *Input* and an *Output* instruction. Notice that when the applet inputs, you are supposed to type a binary number in the *Input* box (which turns yellow) and press *Return*. The program will output the number you entered.

3) Now we'll modify the program: In place of the STP instruction in word 2, encode a STO (store) instruction that will store the accumulator value in memory cell 10.

4) Since you replaced the STP instruction in Step 3 above, you should create a new STP instruction in word 3, to make sure your program halts.

5) Run your program. When it finishes, you should see your input number in the memory cell labeled 10.

6) Take a screenshot of your program.

Exercise 3

Name _____   Date _____

Section _____

1) Start the "Super simple CPU" applet, or press the *Reset* and *Clear Mem* buttons if it's already running.

2) Type the following instructions into memory cells 0 and 1. (The 16-bit numbers are broken with spaces to make them easier to read. **Do not put spaces in your numbers when you type them in!**)

> 0100 0000 0000 1110
>
> 0011 0000 0000 1110

3) In cell 14, type the following:

> 0000 0000 0001 0101

4) Run the program by single-stepping. Press the "1 step" button. After the first instruction finishes (the blue box will say "Updating PC"), write down its three-letter mnemonic and the value in the accumulator.

LDI

0000 0000 0000 1110

5) Press "1 step" again to run the second instruction and write down the mnemonic and the accumulator's value.

LOD

0000 0000 0001 0101

6) Take a screenshot.

7) Explain the difference between the two instructions. (Hint: They are both loading instructions which means they cause a new number to be put into the accumulator. But there is a difference.)

8) Why do you suppose there is no "store immediate" instruction?

9) What sequence of regular instructions could be used to do the same thing? That is, how could we store a specific number, say 129, into a specific memory location, say memory cell 12?

Exercise 4

Name _____   Date _____

Section _____

1) Start the "Super simple CPU" applet.

2) Load the counting loop example (Example 5).

3) Run the applet and write down the PC after each instruction.

4) Take a screenshot and circle all the jumping instructions.

5) Be a human "disassembler." Translate the computer instructions in cells 1 to 5 into mnemonics. Remember, only the first 4 bits of each instruction is the opcode. To see the opcode list, click on the "Opcode list" button.

Mem cell   Mnemonic

0   _____

1   _____

2   _____

3   _____

4   _____

Exercise 5

Name _____ Date _____

Section _____

1) Start the "Super simple CPU" applet.

2) Load the GCD example (Example 6). (A blast from you mathematical past. GCD is short for Greatest Common Divisor.)

3) Run it so you can see that it works. (You might want to speed it up! To do this, pull down the speed list and select "fast.")

4) Click the *Reset* button. Click on the binary checkbox at the bottom of memory so that decimal numbers appear in memory instead of binary. In location 14, type *16* and in location 15 type *28*. What do you think the GCD of these numbers will be?

5) Run the program. When it is done, take a screenshot. Find the memory cell that has the GCD and circle it.

6) What is the GCD of 20 and 21? You could use the applet to confirm your suspicions. Click on these buttons: Stop, Reset. Then type *20* into cell 14, and type *21* into cell 15. Press the *Run* button.

Exercise 6 (This one is challenging!)

Name _____ Date _____

Section _____

1) Start the "Super simple CPU" applet.

2) Load the GCD example (Example 5).

3) *Disassemble* the program in memory. This means write a human-readable version by decoding the instructions.

When writing the program, put the memory address to the left, followed by the two- or three-letter mnemonic for the opcode. Follow that with a number if it is a jump or LDI instruction, or an arithmetic instruction (ADD or SUB). You could go one step further and replace 14 with a variable name of your choosing, and 15 with another variable name. For example, A and B will work.

Here's the disassembled version of example 4 "copy a number":

```
0      LDI    13

1      LOD    13

2      STD    12

3      STP
```

Deliverables

Turn in your hand-written sheets showing your answers to the exercises, along with the screenshots as requested.

Deeper Investigation

We have been very sneaky with the "Super simple CPU" applet. We have taught you some elementary programming! It is hard to examine a programmable device like a computer without talking about programming just a little bit. Perhaps getting your feet wet in this shallow water before officially learning the ins and outs of programming in Chapter 8 lessens the fear, or whets the appetite! Ask any programmer: Sure, programming can be frustrating, infuriating, or irritating at times, but above all, when you get it, *it is fun! Lots of fun!*

If every program is ultimately made up of thousands of individual, simple CPU instructions, as we saw in the "Super simple CPU" applet, what makes software so complex? Let's investigate by analogy, turning to other disciplines.

Think about a field of study that you enjoy: music, chemistry, politics, linguistics, geology. In most fields, there are basic elements out of which more complex things are built. Music has tones and rhythms. Chemistry has atoms and electron valence shells. Where does complexity come from?

For example, in chemistry there are only so many different elements (kinds of atoms), and there are only a few different ways they can attach to one another and stick together. Why, then, are there some 100 thousand compounds?

Write a few paragraphs in which you speculate on how complex things can arise out of combining a few basic elements. How can you put basic elements together to achieve complex systems?

Laboratory

Problem Solving

6

Objective

- Gain experience with Polya's problem-solving methodology.
- Study algorithm development using top-down design and object-oriented design.

References

No software needed (unless you want to use a word processor for writing).

Textbook reference: Chapter 6, pp. 152–186

Background

You should read Chapter 6, "Problem Solving and Algorithm Design," thoroughly and study the examples of algorithm design it contains.

Activity

Algorithm design using reliable and disciplined methodologies was not done in the early days of computing. Programmers learned from each other, from studying someone else's code, and just by sheer intelligence and fortitude. But in the 1960s, when software projects started to balloon to millions of lines of code, this lack of clear methods prompted people to invent methodologies. Top-down design was one of the earliest. Object-oriented design became prevalent by the late 1980s and early 1990s with widespread use of C++ and other object-oriented languages.

However, designing solutions to problems using computers has always remained difficult. Because computers are used to solve such a wide variety of problems, there isn't one perfect recipe for cooking up a suitable program. However, there are some guidelines and strategies, which are discussed thoroughly in Chapter 6 of your textbook.

This lab is an exercise in thinking, discussing, and writing. No computer software is involved, unless you care to write using a word processor. Follow the directions and consult your textbook frequently. It might be good to work with another person, or even with a small group, because different people read different things in the problem and thus allow you to gain a wider perspective.

Exercise 1

Name _____ Date _____

Section _____

1) Suppose that you have been asked to write an algorithm, which will ultimately be implemented on a computer, to plan a vacation for a family traveling by car. The family wants to visit a number of cities in order to see relatives, to see historical attractions, and to have lots of fun at an amusement park. Write down all the items of information that the computer will need. (Hint: Think about money, time, and routes.)

2) What would a solution look like? What should the computer deliver as output to the family?

3) Is there one perfect solution, or might the family like to choose from several solutions? What would the trade-offs between different solutions likely be?

4) Let's now apply top-down design to this problem. Here's the top-level main module:

> Ask for a starting city and destination. Then find routes between them with associated costs. Choose the best routes.

Decompose this by attaching some boxes underneath it that give the main phases of solving the algorithm.

5) One of the difficulties of translating a top-down design written with charts or pseudo-code into a computer program is recognizing which of the actions you list can be done directly by the computer, and which need further refining and breaking down into more primitive actions. Which of the actions in the list below sound like they might be "doable" by present-day computers?

- Find a highway route from Philadelphia to New York.

- Add the hotel cost to the running total of how much money has been spent.

- Ask the family what city they are starting their trip from.

- Order tickets for the amusement park.

- Put gas into the car's tank.

- Print a list of cities in the order in which they should be visited.

- Book a hotel room in New York by e-mail.

- Sort the list of cities by priority number.

- Decide whether more historical attractions than amusement parks should be visited.

- Look up the distance from city A to city B.

6) Suppose you have a distance table that gives the distance between any two cities, such as the one shown below. If there is no number in the intersection, the cities are not directly connected by a road. (All cities and distances are purely fictitious.)

	Alcrombie	Balooska	Chimichanga	Del Roy Point	Eberley
Alcrombie		50	87	20	
Balooska	50			39	77
Chimichanga	87			12	
Del Roy Point	20	39	12		100
Eberley		77		100	

Try to write a pseudo-code algorithm that takes in the name of two cities and finds a route between them. You will need to use a `while` loop (see textbook pp. 257–258 and 257). You can also check off names on the table.

What kinds of pitfalls lie in wait for your algorithm? What kinds of special cases would it have to deal with?

How could you test your algorithm without actually jumping in the car and driving the proposed route?

Exercise 2

Name _____ Date _____

Section _____

1) You have so many music CDs now that you no longer know what you have, where they are, or who has borrowed them. The other day at the mall you bought a really cool CD, only to discover back at home that you already owned it. That's it! Time to get organized.

Use object-oriented design to design a program that will let you keep track of your collection. First, use brainstorming and filtering (textbook p. 179) to begin discovering what classes you need.

Below is the beginning of a description of the required program. Complete it with a reasonable amount of detail. (See the bottom of p. 171 in your textbook for the address list example.)

```
Create a CD catalog that includes all of my CDs with information
about what music is on them,...
```

2) Circle the nouns and underline the verbs in your completed description.

3) Pick out three classes from the above description and fill out the following CRC cards (see textbook pp. 180–183). At this point, focus mostly on the class name and the responsibilities.

Class Name:	Superclass:		Subclass:
Responsibilities		Collaborations	

Class Name:	Superclass:		Subclass:
Responsibilities		Collaborations	

Class Name:	Superclass:		Subclass:
Responsibilities		Collaborations	

4) Classes are related in one of three ways: *containment, inheritance,* or *collaboration* (textbook pp. 173–174). Next to each of the following pairs of classes, write the name of the appropriate relationship.

_____   engine   automobile

_____   mechanic   automobile

_____   4-wheel vehicle   automobile

5) Now do the same for several of the classes that you identified in your CD catalog problem. Try to find one example of each relationship.

6) Choose a class from your CD catalog problem and answer the following questions related to information hiding, abstraction, and naming things (textbook pp. 186–188). You may use a different class for each question.

a) What details are irrelevant to your program and should be omitted?

b) List a class that you have named, but that does not really have a physical existence as one thing. (For example, a *nation* is a collection of people and institutions; a *sports team* is a collection of people. We often think of nations and teams as real things, but what happens when one of its parts leaves? Is it still the same thing?)

c) Identify some action (responsibility) for a class that is a procedural abstraction. That is, it represents a lot of smaller actions.

Deeper Investigation

So far in the history of computing, people have written algorithms and programs, and computers have executed them. Computers devise solutions only in a few vary narrow subfields. Why do you suppose this is so? What is it about solving a problem, devising a plan, and writing an algorithm that is so hard that only humans usually do it?

Suppose that in the year 2052 computers routinely consult with humans who need a problem solved. The computers carry on some sort of conversation with the human, and then write the algorithm and execute it. What kinds of skills will computers need to do this 50 years down the road? What kinds of skills will humans need to be understandable? What are some of the dangers and pitfalls of having computers solve problems and write programs, instead of humans?

Laboratory

Low-Level Languages

7

Objective

- Study simple machine language and assembly language programs.

References

Software needed:

1) A web browser (Internet Explorer or Netscape)

2) Applet from the CD-ROM:

   a) Super simple CPU

Textbook reference: Chapter 7, pp. 201–223

Background

Chapter 7, "Low-Level Programming Languages," discusses the basic concepts of machine and assembly programming. In this lab, we will use the same "Super simple CPU" applet that we used in Lab 5 (instead of Pep/7 that is discussed in the textbook). You should review Lab 5 for basic instructions on how to use the Super Simple CPU.

Activity

In Chapter 5, we studied the fetch-execute cycle while watching the Super simple CPU run a few programs. In this lab, we will look at a further refinement; assembler programming.

To begin, start the applet and click on the *Assembler Window* button. When the window appears, choose *Sequence* from the menu. This puts a short assembler program in the left window. Now click on *Assemble*. Here's what you should see:

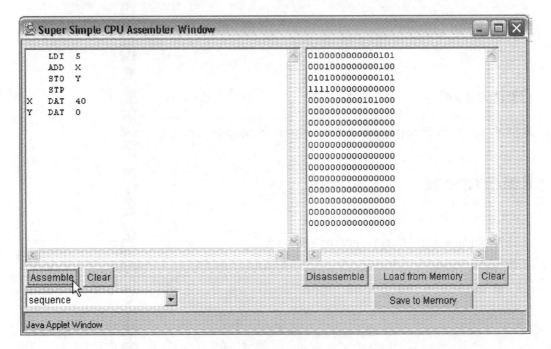

The machine language equivalent of the assembler program appears in the right window. Since there are 16 words in the memory of the Super simple CPU, the assembler creates sixteen 16-bit values, one per memory word, padded out with 0s as necessary to make up 16 bits.

Assembler language (also called assembly language) is the human-readable encoding of machine language instructions. There is one assembler line per machine language instruction. The Super simple CPU is so basic and small that one instruction can fit neatly into just one memory word. As discussed in Lab 5, the first four bits are the opcode and the last 12 bits are the operand (see Lab 5 if you need a reminder).

Also remember from Lab 5 that you can see what the numerical 4-bit opcodes are and what they do from the help buttons on the main window of the applet, or from the opcode list in this manual on p. 69.

To demonstrate how machine language can be translated into assembler language, we'll start with the first machine language instruction that appears in the program we loaded into the CPU applet:

```
0100000000000101
```

(Believe it or not, many early programmers, including some still alive today, programmed computers in lines of binary machine language code just like this. Imagine how tricky it is to create, and especially to debug, a large program in machine language! That's exactly why assembler language was invented around 1952.)

Let's decode this instruction. First, assembler language replaces the four-digit opcode with its three-letter *mnemonic* (this strangely spelled word—the leading "m" is silent—comes from a Greek word meaning "to remember").

Looking up 0100 from the opcode list, we see it corresponds to LDI, the load immediate instruction. So the assembler language instruction should begin with LDI. Next, we convert the 12-digit binary operand (000000000101) into decimal, which gives us 5. So the complete assembler language equivalent of

```
0100000000000101
```

is LDI 5.

(If you wish, you can specify the operand as a binary number instead of a decimal number in the assembler code. However, to keep the Super simple CPU from getting confused as to whether 10 is "two" or "ten," you must put a b (or B) after a binary number. So, you could also have written LDI 101b and the applet would translate it into exactly the same machine instruction. Unlike the machine language instruction, you don't need to pad out the front of 101b with 0s.)

From what we've seen so far, assembler language is merely a straightforward translation of machine language, easier to read, certainly, but of limited usefulness. The real power comes when addresses are encoded symbolically, using *identifiers*. An identifier is a descriptive word or phrase used by the programmer to aid in understanding the role of a memory address or data. That identifier is then used instead of referencing the memory address. Unlike opcodes, which are a defined set of instructions, a programmer can make up the identifiers to suit the situation—for example, you can replace numerical memory addresses with meaningful identifiers such as SALARY or TOPOFLOOP or SALESTAX. With identifiers, it's easier to understand the purpose of a line of code.

Let's look at a simple loop program, one that loads 20 into the accumulator, checks to see if it is 0, subtracts 1 if not, and continues. Close the assembler window, returning to the main window. Pull down *Example 5* from the examples menu.

Here's the program that will load into memory (the opcodes are separated from the operands here just to make it easier to read):

```
0100 000000010100
1001 000000000100
0010 000000000101
1000 000000000001
1111 000000000000
0000 000000000001
```

Even with the opcodes and operands separated, it's still not easy to decipher what this program does.

Click on *Assembler Window* in the main applet screen again. Once you see it, click on *Load from Memory*, as shown below:

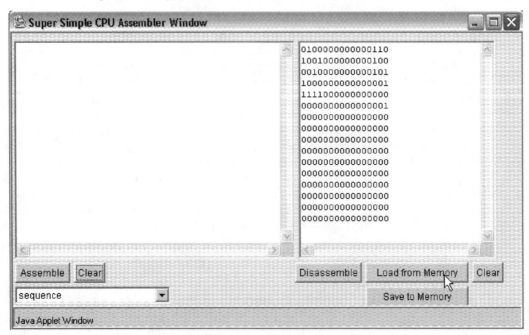

This copies the memory values from the Super simple CPU's memory into the machine language area of the assembler window. Now click on *Disassemble*, and let's see how smart the Super Simple CPU is. Can it reconstruct the original assembler program or not?

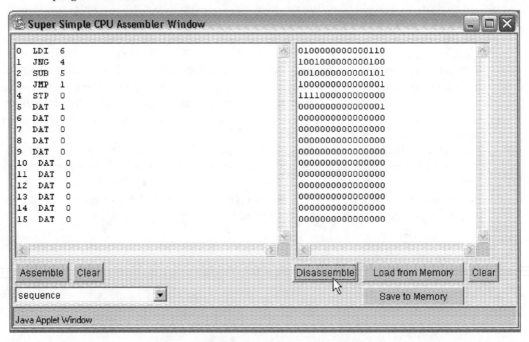

And the answer is ... well, not really. Sure, the *Disassemble* button translated the opcodes into mnemonics and converted the operands to decimal, but it left the addresses as they are. For example, the second instruction, JNG 4, jumps to memory word 4 if the accumulator is negative. But what is at word 4? A STP instruction, which will stop the computer. So address 4 could be better represented with an identifier that tells what its function is, like DONE or ENDOFLOOP.

Let's take a look at a version of this program in assembler that takes full advantage of the power of identifiers to create an easier-to-understand program. First, click on the two *Clear* buttons to clear your assembler windows. Then pull down the menu to *Counting Loop.*

The assembler program that appears in the left text area (shown below), is *much* more readable than the previous version—once you understand how assembler language uses identifiers.

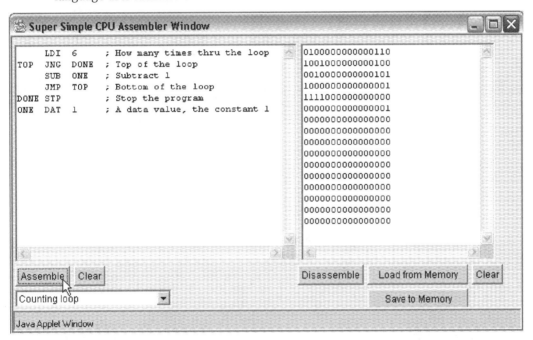

To help you understand how assembler language uses identifiers, the chart below goes step by step through each line of the machine language version of this program, showing its corresponding assembler language version and explaining the identifiers used.

Memory Location	Machine Language Instruction	Assembly Language Instruction
0	0100000000010100 Load 20 into the accumulator.	LDI 20 LDI: The opcode. 20: The value contained in the operand, which should be loaded into the accumulator.
1	1001000000000100 Jump to memory location 4 if the value in the accumulator is < 0.	TOP JNG DONE TOP: Identifier given to this memory location, since it represents the top of a loop that first examines the contents of the accumulator to see if it is < 0. JNG: The opcode. DONE: The identifier given to memory location 4 (see next page).

2	001000000000101 Subtract the value in memory location 5 from the accumulator.	SUB ONE SUB: The opcode. ONE: Instead of referring to memory location 5, this instruction refers to an identifier called ONE (see below). Since ONE has a defined value of 1, 1 will be subtracted from the accumulator.
3	100000000000001 Jump to the instruction at memory location 1.	JMP TOP JMP: The opcode. TOP: Instead of referring to memory location 1, it refers to the identifier TOP. At this point the program jumps up to the top of the loop.
4	111100000000000 Stop the program.	DONE STP DONE: Identifier given to this memory location, since it contains the instruction to stop the program. STP: The opcode.
5	000000000000001 The value 1 is stored in this memory location, to be referred to by the program as needed.	ONE DAT 1 ONE: Identifier for this chunk of data, since it has the value of 1. DAT: This is not one of the opcodes; instead, it is a *pseudo-op* that tells the assembler software that this is data. 1: The value of the data that is to be linked to the identifier ONE.

Let's look at that final line of the assembler program:

```
ONE DAT 1
```

It doesn't create a machine instruction, because there is no machine opcode for DAT. Instead, DAT is what is known as a *pseudo-op*, a directive that is meaningful for the assembler software but that does not correspond to an opcode command.

Here, ONE DAT 1 instructs the assembler to change the decimal number 1 into binary, store it into memory, and link the identifier ONE to the address of that word. DAT is called an assembler *pseudo-op* because there is no corresponding opcode called DAT. Rather, DAT is a directive for the assembler software, telling it what to do. Real assemblers have many pseudo-ops.

Click on *Assemble*, and the equivalent machine language program appears in the right text area, identical to what we saw before.

Writing assembler programs is an art as well as a craft. There are many different identifiers that can be used in place of machine addresses, but some make more sense than others. As with all programs, assembler programs should be written with *documentation* that will help future programmers decipher and modify the code, because useful programs undergo constant mutation as ever-greater demands are made on them. As the old programmer's lament goes: "If the program works, it must be changed!"

Exercise 1

Name _____ Date _____

Section _____

1) Start the "Super simple CPU" applet.

2) Open the Assembler Window.

3) Load the GCD example and take a screenshot.

4) On your screenshot, draw arrows from the jumping instructions to their *target addresses*.

5) Change the second line from the bottom to read A DAT 21; A = 21 and change the bottom line to read B DAT 14; B = 14.

6) Click *Assemble*, then click *Save to Memory*. Go back to the main window.

7) Trace the program. In other words, pretend you are the computer and do one instruction at a time, writing down the values in IR and ACC at the end of each fetch-execute cycle.

First, note the number in the PC, then click on the *1 Step* button. When that step finishes running, note the decoded IR (the mnemonic value in the box just beneath the IR box) and the value in the accumulator. Start a new line for the next step, noting the PC first, then once again clicking the *1 Step* button and noting the resulting IR and ACC values. Continue until the program is finished.

To get you started, here are the first few lines of the trace done for you as an example. You should make sure that your results match these as you start out:

PC	IR	ACC
0	LOD 14	21
1	SUB 15	7
2	JZR 10	7
3	JNG 6	7
5	STO 14	7
6	JMP 0	7
0	LOD 14	...

8) Now click on *Log Window* and compare your trace with what the computer did as it ran the program. Did you get the same results? (We assume the computer was right, because, as everyone knows, computers *never* make mistakes!)

Exercise 2

Name _____   Date _____

Section _____

1) Start the "Super simple CPU" applet. Select *Example 3* (*Negative numbers*) from the pull-down menu.

2) Open the assembler window, click on *Load from Memory*, and then click *Disassemble*.

3) Take a screenshot of the assembler window.

4) Rewrite the assembler program, removing unneeded DAT lines and replacing addresses with identifiers. Be careful—there's a trap here! Several instructions shouldn't have identifiers as operands. Can you spot them? (Hint: Study the assembler program shown on the screenshot on the very first page of this lab as a model for what you are to do here. Make sure you understand what that program does and how it uses identifiers.)

Exercise 3

Name _____   Date _____

Section _____

1) Start the "Super simple CPU" applet.

2) Click on the "Assemble window" button. This brings up a blue window with several large text areas and some buttons.

3) In the left text area, type the following program. Make sure to put some spaces in front of the instruction mnemonic if there is no label. This means, for example, to hit the space bar several times before typing the "INP" in the first line.

```
        INP
        STO   A
        SUB   FIVE
        JZR   SHOW1
SHOW0   LDI 0
        OUT
        STP
SHOW1   LDI 1
        OUT
        STP
A       DAT   0
FIVE    DAT   5
```

4) Click on the Assemble button in the blue window. What do you see in the right text area? Can you make the correspondence between the mnemonics in the left text area with the binary codes in the right?

5) To transfer this program into the memory of the Super simple CPU, click on the button "Save to Memory." Close the blue window. Notice the binary version of the program has been copied into the memory cells. (The program is still there even though the blue window is invisible. Just click on "Assemble window" again to see it.)

6) Run the program. The first instruction will ask you for input. Type in 101, since the Super simple CPU requires your input to be binary. What is the output?

7) Click on Reset and Run the program again. This time, type in 111 and write down what the output is.

8) Look at the previous program and trace through the instructions. Imagine that you typed in 101. Circle all the instructions that are executed when this is what you inputted. Here's another copy of the program to mark up.

```
        INP
        STO  A
        SUB  FIVE
        JZR  SHOW1
SHOW0   LDI  0
        OUT
        STP
SHOW1   LDI  1
        OUT
        STP
A       DAT  0
FIVE    DAT  5
```

9) Two fundamental control structures in computer programming are *decisions* and *loops*. Does this program contain a decision? If so, which instructions trigger the taking of an alternate path?

10) Does this program contain a loop? If so, where is the instruction that causes the computer to jump back to an earlier spot?

Deliverables

Turn in your hand-written sheets for the questions requiring written answers. Also turn in the screenshots requested in the exercises.

Deeper Investigation

We have seen how the assembler software (which is part of the "Super Simple CPU" applet here, but is usually separate) translates assembler programs into machine language. Some of this process is straightforward, but some is not.

Think about what has to be done when translating the identifiers that replace memory addresses. How does the assembler do it? Would a table of identifier/address pairs be helpful? What happens to *forward references*? This refers to identifiers that are used as operands before we know what they turn into, as in the following:

```
    LOD  A
    ADD  B
    STO  C
    STP
A   DAT  26
B   DAT  19
C   DAT  0
```

There are actually three forward references here, to A, B, and C.

Try to describe the algorithm that the assembler might use to translate an assembler program into machine language. Just use English to write your algorithm; by no means should you try to do it in assembler language!

Laboratory

8

Using Algorithms for Painting

Objectives

- Learn how to use Palgo, an applet that *Paints ALGO*rithmically.
- Learn how to write programs for Palgo.

References

Software needed:

1) A web browser (Internet Explorer or Netscape)

2) Applet from the CD-ROM:

   a) Palgo

Textbook reference: Chapter 8

Background

The general background of high-level programming languages is presented in Chapter 8. Palgo uses an imperative programming language to draw pictures. The language constructs are explained in this lab.

Activity

Sometimes it is hard to get a feel for algorithms when solving traditional problems, such as sorting a list or averaging employees' salaries. Pictures are "funner!" Palgo follows in a long tradition, starting with Seymour Papert's Turtle Graphics, of using a programming language to draw pictures. All the basic elements of algorithms can be used and studied: sequence, decision, repetition, and subalgorithm.

To begin, start the "Palgo" applet. The edit window will appear, with the painting window behind it. Select *Example 1* (*Simple Square*) from the pull-down menu, and press the *Run* button. In the painting window you'll see a square, with four different-colored sides (see the screenshot below).

This first program is quite simple, consisting only of a sequence of painting commands. The `color` command changes the color of the invisible pen that is drawing on the square. The `pen down` and the `pen up` commands tell Palgo to start or stop coloring squares with the current color, respectively. (You would need to stop painting, for example, if you wanted the pen to jump to a non-adjacent square without painting the intervening squares.)

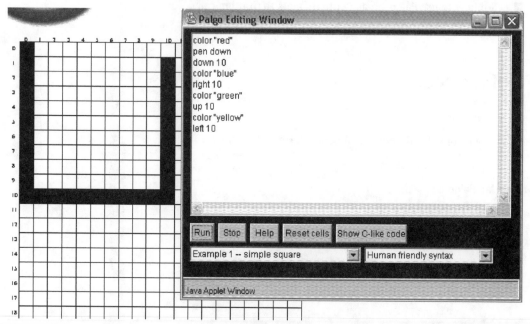

The invisible pen starts out pointing to square 0,0 in the upper left corner. (We will denote squares by a comma-separated pair of numbers, where the first number is the column and the second is the row. Thus square 0,1 is the leftmost yellow square in the above picture, and 10,9 is the rightmost blue square.)

Palgo has four commands for moving the pen around: `up`, `down`, `left`, and `right`. If the pen is down, it paints into the square beneath it and any squares it passes over. If it is up, it can move over squares without painting them. The four direction commands can have a number parameter, such as 10 in the program above. This means to move 10 squares in the direction indicated, all the while painting the squares if the pen is down.

Though a sequential program like the one above can look rather complicated and can draw a pretty picture, the real power of Palgo appears when you use control structures. Click *Reset cells*, then select *Example 4—squares* from the pull-down menu, and click *Run*. Watch what happens in the painting window.

Here's the program, along with an explanation of how it works (the line numbers to the left are for reference only—they do not appear in the actual program):

```
1. define square (n)
2.      pen down
3.      down n
4.      right n
5.      up n
6.      left n
7. end
8. goto 0 0
9. color "red"
10. square(10)
11. goto 2 2
12. color "yellow"
13. square(4)
14. goto 12 12
15. color "blue"
16. square(5)
```

The first seven lines define a subalgorithm called *square*. The identifier n inside parentheses on the define line (line 1) is the parameter to *square*. (The textbook introduces parameters on pp. 260–264. Palgo has only *value* parameters.)

Line 8 directs the pen to go to position 0,0 in the upper left corner. Line 9 sets the current color to "red," and then line 10 *invokes* the subalgorithm named square, telling it to substitute the number 10 for its parameter n. As you might guess from reading the code inside the *square* subalgorithm, the parameter tells Palgo how big to draw the sides of the square.

After changing starting position and color in lines 11–12, the program invokes *square* again, asking it to draw a smaller square in line 13. Then a 5-unit square is drawn by line 16.

Compare the code in the edit window with the results in the painting window, and make sure you understand how the program works.

Now we'll take a look at a different program. Select *Example 3—random colored dots*. Press *Reset cells*, then press *Run*. Let the program go for a while, noting what happens, then read on.

Palgo has several ways to repeat sections of code. One is to surround the code with `repeat X times` and `end`. (The end keyword is used in Palgo for all control structures, in order to mark the end of their influence. We saw this with the `define` construct above.) To cause one or several lines to be executed many times, simply tuck them inside a repeat loop. The number of times can be either a constant, such as 1000 in this example, or a variable.

The code inside a repeat loop is called the *body* of the loop. This is the code that is performed over and over until the loop stops. *If* statements, as well as subalgorithm *define* statements, also have bodies. Notice that in our examples these bodies are indented to set them apart from the rest of the code. This indenting doesn't affect the way the code runs, but experienced programmers use indenting to help make their code more readable.

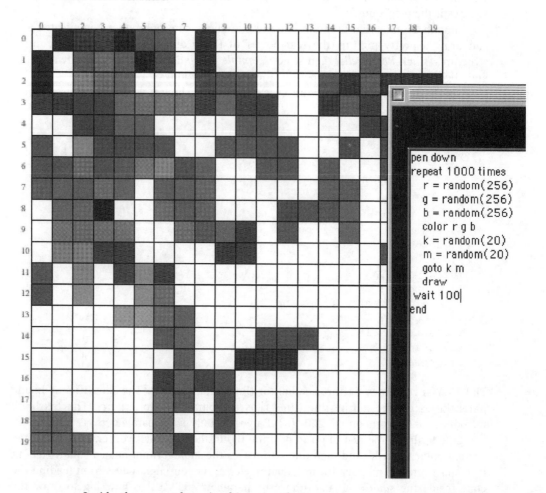

```
pen down
repeat 1000 times
    r = random(256)
    g = random(256)
    b = random(256)
    color r g b
    k = random(20)
    m = random(20)
    goto k m
    draw
    wait 100|
end
```

Inside the repeat loop in this example is a sequence of simple Palgo statements, but there could have been `if` statements or even other repeat loops. Early computer scientists must have had a love for biology, even well before bioinformatics caught on, because much of the terminology of computer science is based on animal and plant metaphors. In this case, a repeat loop sitting inside the body of another repeat loop is said to be *nested*.

There are a few interesting things worth noting in the sequential body of our example. First is the use of a built-in function called `random()`. This pulls a random number that is 256 units wide out of a hat. Actually, it creates what is called a pseudo-random number, one that is based on some mathematical principle such as doing complicated and contorted divisions and additions, but that looks pretty random. The parameter to the built-in function, 256, tells Palgo to generate a random number between 0 and 255, inclusive.

Why use 256 as the parameter? As you might recall from Lab 3B, "Colorful Characters," the answer has to do with how computers represent colors. 256 is 2^8, and there are 8 bits per primary color. Each color is represented by three 8-bit numbers, called red, green, and blue. Many millions of colors can be produced by this scheme, which is discussed in the textbook on pages 77–81.

This Palgo program generates three random values for the red, green, and blue components. Then it makes the color by the statement

```
color r g b
```

Remember that since the names `r`, `g`, and `b` are not surrounded by double quotes, Palgo thinks of them as variables that contain integer values. In contrast, the statement `color "red"` sets the current color to red directly. But many of the approximately 16 million possible colors in the red-green-blue scheme do not have simple names like this, so sometimes we specify the color by numbers.

After we generate a random color, we generate a random position. Because our painting window consists of a square 20 cells to a side, we use `random(20)`. Then we go to that newly calculated spot with

```
goto k m
```

and paint the square. This command dips the invisible pen in the magical electronic inkwell and dabs the splash of color onto the screen. Finally, we wait for a short amount of time (100 milliseconds) before starting the whole thing over. Try changing the `wait` value from 100 to 10 and see if your screen doesn't get painted faster when you run the program.

Does it surprise you that seemingly simple painting tasks have rather involved algorithms behind them? This example points out how complex computer programming is, even for "simple" tasks. The computer, an untiring, uncomplaining slave, might make its way through thousands (or even millions) of lines of tedious code just to execute a seemingly simple drawing. (Of course, since this slave might be doing a billion calculations a second, I guess we'd better give it some respect!)

Let's look at a more complicated program, "Example 6 - red and yellow." Here's a screenshot of the program while it's running:

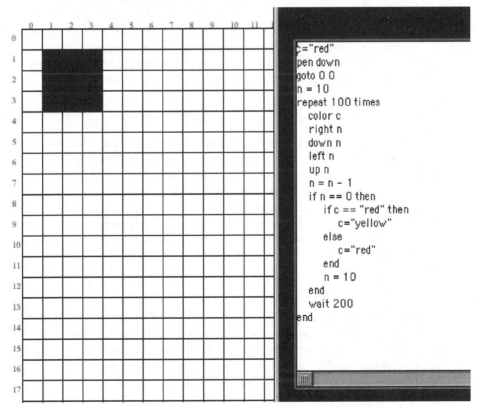

```
c="red"
pen down
goto 0 0
n = 10
repeat 100 times
    color c
    right n
    down n
    left n
    up n
    n = n - 1
    if n == 0 then
        if c == "red" then
            c="yellow"
        else
            c="red"
        end
        n = 10
    end
    wait 200
end
```

This program, which draws a succession of red and yellow shrinking boxes, has two important variables, whose identifiers are c and n. (Way too many of us older computer scientists grew up in the ancient FORTRAN era, when one-letter variable names were considered absolutely okay.) c holds a string, which is either "red" or "yellow" in this program. When it comes time to dip the invisible pen in the magical inkwell, the statement

```
color c
```

tells Palgo which color to use.

The variable n is used to determine the size of one side of the square being drawn. It starts out at 10 and then progressively gets smaller by using the statement

```
n = n - 1
```

An if statement inside the body of the loop checks to see if n's value is 0, because if it is, the program needs to swap colors and reset the size of the square side to 10.

One rather strange bit of hieroglyphics is the line

```
if n == 0 then
```

Did the programmer stutter at the keyboard? No, this statement is influenced by another bit of computer history. First, notice the line

```
n = n - 1
```

This looks weird, too, until you realize that this is not an algebraic statement of equality but rather an action command. It tells Palgo to evaluate the right-hand side of the equal sign and come up with a value, then stash that into the variable on the left-hand side. Such an action command is called an *assignment statement*, and the equal sign is the *assignment operator*.

Since = is the assignment operator, it can't be used for ordinary equality because computers, unlike humans, are terrible at using the context to determine what is meant. (No wonder computers are horrible at understanding French, German, or English!) Thus, ==, which is pronounced "equals," is used for ordinary equality.

Equals (==) functions as a *comparative operator*, meaning "is equal to". So the statement if n == 0 then translates into "if n equals 0 then ...". This is different from =, which as an assignment operator assigns a value to a variable—so in the statement n = n - 1, the variable n decreases by 1. (You already know several other comparative operators: > for "is greater than" and < for "is less than" are two examples.)

Let's see, didn't we mention some computer science history? Actually, several lines of history intersect here. The assignment operator, first used in FORTRAN, should really have been something more meaningful (like a left-pointing arrow, perhaps), but the IBM 026 keypunch machine commonly in use at the time only had a few symbols on it, and John Backus, who headed the FORTRAN compiler team, had to make do with what they had. In the 1970s, when Brian Kernighan and Dennis Ritchie created the C programming language, they were faced with the same sort of problem and, being familiar with FORTRAN, decided to retain the assignment operator as is. However, they hated the ugly symbol that FORTRAN used for testing equality, which was .EQ., as in:

```
IF(X.EQ.5) GOTO 76
```

so they humanely chose == for equality testing. Their reasoning was clever. They believed that the assignment operator would appear about twice as often as the comparative operator, so it should be half as long. (Some linguists believe that the most frequently used words in human languages are almost always the shortest words.)

Enough computer science history and lore! There are a few other aspects of Palgo you should become familiar with.

Click the *Show C-like code* button. This displays a different form of the program, in a yellow window you can resize and reposition for more convenient viewing:

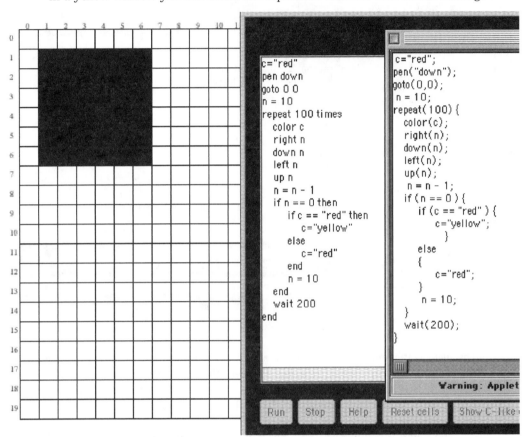

Palgo uses software tools to translate and execute programming language code. These tools include a crucial piece called the *parser*. You might be surprised to learn that the original parser was written to interpret a C-like programming language, replete with those scary curly braces and abundant semicolons. The applet author, realizing how cruel it is to force you to program in C, wrote a translator that permits the use of "human-friendly syntax," which is then converted into this C-like language to be used by the parser. (In fact, you can use the C-like syntax if you select *C-style syntax* from the pull-down menu choice at the bottom of the edit window. (You probably won't want to try it, though, unless you have some programming experience or are a glutton for punishment!) This illustrates the power and beauty of software; it is infinitely adaptable, reusable, and malleable.

Finally, as you saw above, Palgo has variables that can be used to compute many things—even some things not involving painting at all. Pull down *Example 7—GCD* and study the code. Notice that it uses no painting commands, but rather computes the greatest common divisor of two numbers that you give it.

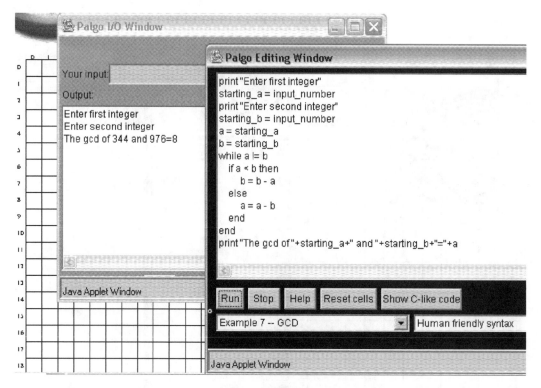

The *print* statement and the *input* statement cause an orange window to appear. When the program asks for input, type any value in the small text area at the top and press *Return*. It is *very important* to press Return, because Palgo doesn't know you are done typing until you actually press the *Return* key. Any output appears in the larger text area below.

The Palgo function `input()` needs no parameters, but the empty parentheses are needed so that Palgo can tell this is a function. The `input()` function returns a character string. Inside your program, you must convert that string to a number by using the `atoi()` function (`atoi` stands for "ASCII to Integer" and is another tip of the hat to the C programming language), as shown above. Then the result of these nested functions is stored in a variable:

```
starting_a = atoi(input())
```

So Palgo can be used to do "regular," non-graphical programming too. Of course, you can also mix the two. Sometimes you need to do a lot of "regular" calculations to figure out where to put the pen. Palgo is a relatively bare-bones graphics system, but if you experiment with writing programs in it, you can become quite familiar with the concept of algorithms.

Tip

Palgo can be used as a standalone Java application. If you use Palgo as an application (not as an applet), you can load and save your programs. To run the Java application, navigate to the folder containing the Palgo files and double-click on the **run-application.bat** file.

Exercise 1

Name _____   Date _____

Section _____

As you work on the following steps, refer to the sample programs for models of what your Palgo programs should look like.

1) Start the "Palgo" applet.

2) In the editing window, type in a sequence of Palgo instructions. Here's what they should do:

   a) Set the color to red.

   b) Draw a line from 2,7 to 2,17.

   c) Set the color to green.

   d) Draw a vertical line starting at 2,7 that is 15 cells long, going down the screen.

3) Click on the *Run* button to run the program.

4) Arrange the edit and painting windows so they're both visible, then take a screenshot.

   Hint: To draw a line, go to the beginning cell. Then use right, down, left, or right for as many cells as needed. For example, to draw a vertical line from the bottom of the cell grid to the top in the second column, use the following commands:

   > color "red"
   >
   > goto 1 19
   >
   > up 20

   Note: Since the rows and columns are numbered starting at 0 instead of 1, the first column is numbered 0, the second column is numbered 1, and so on.

Exercise 2

Name _____ Date _____

Section _____

1) Start the "Palgo" applet.

2) Select *Example 4—squares* from the pull-down menu.

3) In the editing window, you will alter the program as follows—but make sure to leave the definition of the square subalgorithm at the top unchanged!

4) Here's how you should alter the program:

   a) Remove everything after the square subalgorithm (the subalgorithm ends with the word end).

   b) Set the variable k to 1.

   c) Write a repeat loop that executes 10 times.

   d) Inside the loop, set the color to a random r, g, b value. This is shown on p. 106 of this lab manual.

   e) Use the goto statement to move to cell k,k in the grid.

   f) Invoke the square algorithm using variable k. This will create a square of size k. The first time through, when k is 1, the square will be 1 × 1. The second time through, the square will be 2 × 2, and so forth.

   g) Add 1 to variable k.

5) Run your program. Take a screenshot showing both the squares and the edit window.

Exercise 3

Name _____ Date _____

Section _____

1) Start the "Palgo" applet or clear it if it is already running.

2) Set the color to blue.

3) Using goto and up, down, right, and left statements, create the following letters side by side:

   T H E

4) Take a screen shot, showing both the Palgo window as well as the cell grid after you run the program.

Exercise 4

Name _____ Date _____

Section _____

1) Start the "Palgo" applet or clear it if it is already running.

2) Type in the following program. (Make sure there are spaces between "draw," "i," and "k")

```
clear
color "orange"
k = 6
for i=3 to 10
      draw i k
      k = k + 1
end
```

3) What kind of line did this draw?

4) Be bold! Change the statement that alters k's value so that it goes up by 2 each time through the for loop. Rerun the program and take a screen shot. Is the new image a line or not?

5) Now change the for loop so that it looks like the following then rerun.

```
for i=3 to 10
      goto i k
      down 2
      k = k + 2
end
```

6) Compare this image to the last one. Which one is more of a line?

7) Most computer screens can't draw freehand like we can. Instead, computers can only paint into little cells, or *pixels*. So drawing lines other than pure horizontal or vertical involves a compromise. If you look at a ragged line from a distance, or if the *resolution* is high (meaning the number of cells in the grid is large), the line will look smoother. Try standing about 10 to 15 feet away from your computer screen and report if the image looks more like a line.

8) Another fun experiment is to get a strong magnifying glass and hold it up to your computer's screen. Look at letters on the screen and report what you see. Also, what do you notice about the colors under the magnifying glass?

9) Palgo lets you change the resolution of your cell grid with the numcells command. Here's a similar program that changes the number of cells from 20 on each size of the grid to 80 on each side. Then it draws a longer line. Run it and take a snapshot.

```
clear
numcells 80
color "orange"
k = 6
for i=3 to 100
    goto i k
    down 2
    k = k + 2
end
```

10) Does the line look smooth enough?

Deliverables

Turn in the screenshot showing your program after it finishes running and the edit window with your program in it.

If you are running Palgo as a standalone Java application, save your file and then print it out. Use a word processor or a text application (like Notepad) to print out the file. Your instructor may ask you to hand in the file electronically, too. Consult the instructor for details on how to do this.

Deeper Investigation

Programming is hard work! As you read through Chapters 8 and 9 of your textbook, you might find yourself working hard to absorb the meaning of while loops, if statements, and subalgorithms. Actually putting your new knowledge into practice and writing real programs is a new, but hopefully fun, challenge. Palgo has the ability to create extremely complicated, program-driven pictures. Play with it and see!

Write a function that draws a filled rectangle. There should be four parameters: starting row, starting column, width, and height. Then cannibalize the random dots program to draw rectangles of random sizes on the screen at random locations, using random colors. (*Cannibalize?* What that means, of course, is to study the code and steal or modify whatever might be useful for your program!)

Laboratory

Abstract Data Types

9A

Objective

■ Gain a deeper appreciation for stacks, queues, and trees.

References

Software needed:

1) A web browser (Internet Explorer or Netscape)

2) Applets

   a) Stackqueue

   b) Trees

Textbook reference: Chapter 9, pp. 286–297

Background

There are many abstract data types in use in Computer Science. Chapter 9 of your textbook covers those most commonly used. In this lab, you will watch stacks, queues, and trees operate in order to gain a deeper understanding of what they look like and how they function. In the next lab, you will investigate how searching and sorting are influenced by the data types used to store values.

Activity

Part 1

Two commonly used abstract data types are stacks and queues, which are similar but are used in very different algorithms. Stacks are probably the most heavily employed workhorses of computing, after lists. This lab allows you to watch both stacks and queues at work.

Start the "Stackqueue" applet. This oddly named applet does not imply that there is a third abstract data type, called a "stackqueue." Rather, the applet combines stacks and queues for convenience' sake. At any given time, the data structure underneath the surface of the applet is either a stack or a queue. By the way, get used to spelling that word (queue.) It isn't really that hard, just remember Q -UE - UE. Two sets of UE and you've won the spelling bee!

The applet starts as a stack that doesn't show itself initially. Click on the *Show* button. Type "cats" into the textfield next to the *Push* button and either press the *Push* button or press the Enter key after typing "cats." This pushes the word onto the stack. Since it is initially empty, "cats" will be the only thing on the stack. Cats like company so push "dogs" onto the stack. Finally push "birds" on. Here's what the applet looks like just before you push "birds" into this happy menagerie:

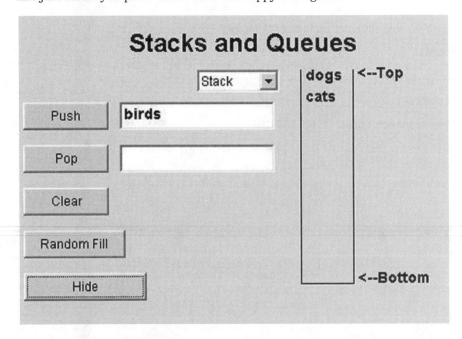

Remember that the first thing you push onto a stack is the last thing that pops out, like the spring-loaded plate well at a cafeteria mentioned on p. 308.

When you click the *Pop* button, the top thing is taken off the stack and appears in the textfield next to the *Pop* button. You can pop everything immediately by pressing *Clear.*

The applet can put a bunch of random numbers on the stack when you press the *Random Fill* button. Though numbers aren't as interesting as animals or names of friends (at least to most people), they are quick and easy to generate randomly.

Clear the stack, and then pull down the menu so that Queue appears. Notice how the picture changes so that there is a Head and Tail, instead of Top and Bottom. Also notice that the queue is open-ended, instead of closed at the bottom, like the stack. The buttons change, too, because Computer Scientists don't like to confuse us by saying that we push things onto queues and pop them off. Rather, they suggest that we enqueue and dequeue, or enter and delete, when using a queue.

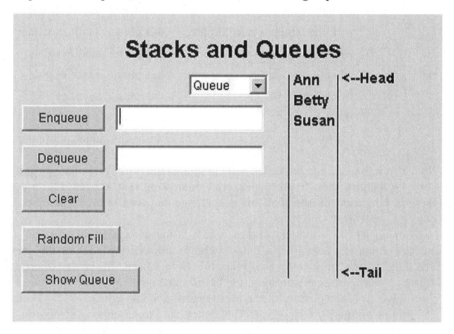

Put three names onto the queue. In the picture above, we enqueued Ann, then Betty, then Susan, in that order. If this were a stack, Ann would be at the bottom and Susan would be at the top. But queues work differently.

When you insert something into a queue, it goes at the end of the line, just like you do when you check out at a grocery store. Whoever is at the head of the line will get checked out next . . . you just have to wait!

What is so different about stacks versus queues? Unfortunately, you will have to learn more about computers and algorithms before you see why both are necessary and not interchangeable. But here are a few hints.

Queues are used in simulations where you generate tasks that you want to finish later or send off to another processor. Operating systems use queues. They often reorder the elements in the queue according to a priority level so that the most important tasks get done first.

Stacks are indispensable to language processing. Researchers believe that we parse sentences by using stacks to remember what phrase modifies which word. Here's an example:

I saw the dog belonging to the girl whom my sister who is studying at the school with the fabulous new library brought with her.

Admittedly, that is kind of awkward, but most English speakers would be able to understand it. They might argue about "whom" or "who," but let's not fight about grammar.

Here's how it works. There are successive levels of phrases and modifiers. Modifying phrases, either prepositional phrases like "at the school" or subordinate clauses like "who is studying . . ." follow the nouns they modify. As an English speaker listens to a sentence like the one above, she picks out the most important structures, and then fits the modifiers in, kind of like pickles and relish on a hamburger, nice but not essential. The attachment of phrases works backward like a stack.

Here's the way many linguists think we figure out the structure. The stack is constructed so that a phrase modifies the thing directly underneath it, in most cases.

top →	brought with _her_.	this is what my sister did
	with the fabulous new library	this phrase modifies school
	who is studying at the school	this phrase modifies sister
	whom my <u>sister</u>	this phrase modifies girl
	belonging to the <u>girl</u>	this phrase modifies dog
	the dog	this is what I saw
	I saw	this is the subject and main verb

Notice how we disambiguate _her_, which could refer to any female, in particular my sister or the girl. Most English speakers would claim that _her_ refers to my sister, not the girl. Linguists contend that this is evidence that we use a mental stack to process complex sentences.

Our applet has a _mystery_ option, which is not some kind of mystical mixture of stacks and queues, but rather a random choice between the stack or the queue. If you are showing the stack or queue, click the _Hide_ button. Otherwise, there's no more mystery. When you select mystery, the buttons change to _Add_ and _Remove_ so that they won't give away the identity of the mystery abstract data type.

Pull down the mystery option. The applet has chosen either a stack or a queue—we don't know which. Press the _Clear_ button to empty it. Now Add "John," then add "Tony."

Here's the fun part. Click on _Remove_. What appears? Is it "John" or "Tony"? What does it mean if it is "John" instead of "Tony"? If you understand the difference between stacks and queues, the answer will be obvious. Just remember LIFO for stacks and FIFO for queues:

LIFO = Last In First Out   Stacks

FIFO = First In First Out   Queues

One last thing. If you try to remove something when the stack or queue is empty, what happens? Also, try to add many things in order to determine the maximum size of the stack or queue. Our applet has a fixed maximum size, but in real applications, programmers can change it.

Part 2

Trees are enormously important, both to provide shade and grow apples and cherries . . . Ooops, wrong trees! The use of the word "tree" to describe the abstract data type that looks more like a root system just shows how upside-down the view of the world as seen by Computer Scientists is. If they start to collaborate with botanists, watch out!

Trees are everywhere in Computer Science. Language processing uses trees, as do compilers of higher level languages like C and Java. You will find binary trees when you examine the playoff schedule for a sports event. Whichever of two teams or contestants who wins moves up the tree to the next level.

Your textbook discusses several types of trees and gives algorithms for examining and changing them. The "Trees" applet allows you to work with a tree and visualize it, but does not permit you to write computer programs to manipulate them. That will come along in later programming courses.

Start the "Trees" applet. Pull down the menu until "Example 1" appears. This creates a tree with five names, as shown below:

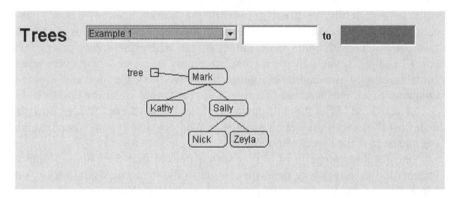

A typical computer program may have many trees, which is sometimes referred to as a "forest" (no kidding, and no logging!) In our applet, there is only one tree, referred to as simply "tree." Notice the little square next to it. That represents the pointer variable that contains the address of the top node, which is occupied by "Mark." Sadly, our applet doesn't have arrows, only lines, but the lines always point down, just like your textbook shows on pages 312–318.

The trees that the examples in this applet create are all binary trees, which means that each node has either no children, one child, or two children. Other trees permit many children. We can also talk about grandchildren nodes, though the term descendant is more common.

A special kind of binary tree is a binary search tree that arranges the nodes in such a way that they can be searched easily. Given a node, all of its left descendants have values that are less than it, numerically or alphabetically. "Kathy" is less than "Mark" because "Kathy" precedes "Mark" in the dictionary, so her node is in the left subtree of "Mark." Similarly, all the right descendants of a node have values greater than the node's data value.

Pull down the menu and select "Insert alphabetically." Then type the name "Liam" into the textfield next to it and press return:

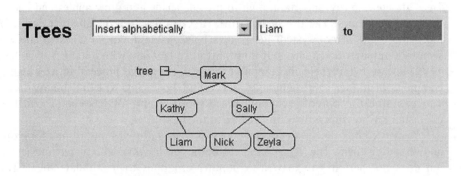

Notice that "Liam" comes between "Kathy" and "Mark" alphabetically. However, the "Mark" node already has two children so it is full. Thus, "Liam" has to go into the left subtree of "Mark." But it can't just replace "Kathy." Instead, "Liam" has to be a child or grandchild, or great-grandchild of "Kathy." Since "Kathy" has no other children at the moment, "Liam" is her right child because "L" comes after "K."

Experiment with some more names to see where the applet places them. If you select Example 3, you will see a complete binary tree, one where every non-leaf node contains exactly two children. Again, this shows how fanciful and upside-down the Computer Science conception of a tree is . . . the leaves are at the bottom?

Select "Find" from the pull-down menu and type "Steve." Watch how some of the nodes turn yellow as the search progresses. You can also type a name that is not in the tree to see how the applet responds.

One fabulous property of binary search trees is that they store a huge amount of information in such a way that you can get to the item you want quickly, unlike a list where you might have to look at everything in list. Notice how the search process descends quickly and doesn't have to look at all the nodes in the tree.

You can attach any node to any existing node in this applet by using one of the two "Attach" options from the pull-down menu. However, this may screw up the alphabetical ordering by doing this. Let's experiment. Select "Clear" and then "Example 1." Now select "Attach as left child" and type "Sheila" in the first textfield and "Kathy" in the second. The second textfield is normally gray so that you can't use it, only becoming usable when you select one of the two "Attach" options.

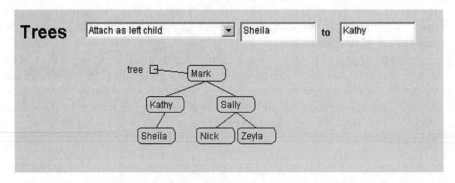

Our tree is still a binary tree, though not a complete one, but it is out of order. Can it find "Sheila" if you search for her? Try it. Why won't it find her?

Exercise 1

Name _____   Date _____

Section _____

1) Start the "Stackqueue" applet.

2) The purpose of this exercise is see how you could reverse a list of names. Push the three names "Abe," "Betty," and "Charles" onto the stack. When you pop the stack 3 times, what do you see in the textfield next to "Pop"?

3) Write an algorithm in pseudo-code or English that would describe how to use a stack to reverse any list. Write your answer below or type it up in a word processor.

4) A palindrome or RADAR word is one that has the same sequence of letters if you read it from right to left or left to right. Describe how you could use a stack in conjunction with the original list to determine if a sequence is a palindrome. Write your answer below or type it up in a word processor. (Hint: Your letters exist in a list. Use one stack and make copies of the letters. Then pop the stack and compare.)

Exercise 2

Name _____   Date _____

Section _____

1) Start the "Stackqueue" applet.

2) The purpose of this exercise is to figure out whether the mystery data structure is a stack or a queue. Click on *Clear*, then *Random Fill*. Select "mystery" from the pull-down menu.

3) Click once on *Remove*. Whatever number appears next to the *Remove* button is what you now type into the textfield next to *Add*. Then click on *Add*.

4) Now click on *Remove*. What value appears? Is it the same one or different? What does this mean? Is your mystery object a stack or a queue? Take a screenshot and write your answer on the paper. You can then *Show* to confirm your conclusion.

Exercise 3

Name _____ Date _____

Section _____

1) Start the "Trees" applet.

2) The purpose of this exercise is to build a binary search tree. Select "Insert alphabetically" from the pull-down menu. Then type the following flowers into the textfield, pressing return after each one.

    Lily

    Rose

    Daffodil

    Tulip

    Petunia

3) Take a screenshot. Now perform a manual search for "Poppy." Put a check mark next to each node that you visit during your search. You can confirm your ideas by selecting "Find" from the pull-down and asking the applet to search for "Poppy."

4) If you were to manually insert "Poppy" into this tree, what would you put into the boxes and which option would you select?

____ "Attach as left child"   _____ to _____

____ "Attach as right child"

Check one blank on the left of "Attach…" and fill in the two blanks surrounding "to."

Exercise 4

Name _____   Date _____

Section _____

1) Start the "Trees" applet.

2) The purpose of this exercise is to build a binary search tree but choosing different orders for inserting the nodes.

3) Type in the following flower names in the given order. (If you don't want to type a lot, just use the first letter of each name.) Take a screenshot when done.

    Aster

    Bluebell

    Coreopsis

    Daisy

    Echinacea

    Fern

    Gladiolus

4) What does your tree look like? Describe it in words below.

5) What generalization can you make about inserting elements from a sorted list into a tree?

6) Could you convince someone that a list is a special kind of tree?

7) Clear the tree and insert the flowers in some other order so that the tree is *balanced* and *complete*. Remember that this means that all nodes except the leaf nodes have exactly two children. After you are successful, take a screenshot. Also write down the exact order that you used to get it to look this way.

8) Is there more than one order that you could have used that would have created the same balanced, complete tree? Why are multiple different orders possible?

Exercise 5

Name _____ Date _____

Section _____

1) Start the "Trees" applet.

2) The purpose of this exercise is to investigate what happens when you have duplicate nodes. Choose "Example 2."

3) Select "Insert Alphabetically." Then type "Mark" in the textfield and press Return. Take a screenshot.

4) Insert another name that is already in the tree. What does this applet do when you ask it to enter a name that is already there?

5) Are there alternative strategies that the applet could have used? List two more.

a) _____

b) _____

6) Does "Find" still work? Try to find a name, like "Mark," that is represented by two nodes. What happens? Describe.

Deliverables

Turn in your hand-written sheets showing your answers to the experiments.

Deeper Investigation

Just as in sorting, there are many search algorithms besides sequential and binary searching. For example, there is the tree searching algorithm presented on p. 315 of your textbook). Think about how you search for a name in a telephone book. You don't need to live in New York City or Los Angeles to realize that *nobody* in their right mind uses sequential search on the telephone book! But just exactly what do people do? What algorithm do they employ? Is it binary search? Can you describe the algorithm in English, even if it is too hard to write out in code?

Think about searching the telephone book again. What kinds of additional information are present to help humans find names in the phone book? How are phone books organized? (Hint: Look at the tops of pages in the phone book.)

Finally, think about finding information in your school's library. You probably have a computer system with an online catalog, but not too long ago, libraries had huge filing cabinets full of 3 × 5 index cards. (In fact, some folks get downright nostalgic for those drawers of musty-smelling cards....) Such indexes now live on (relatively scent-free) computer hard disks.

Think about the steps you would have to go through to find a specific piece of information or a quotation in your library. What indexes would you search? What happens when the index leads you to the book itself? What then? How might all this change in the upcoming years as computerization advances?

Laboratory

Searching for the Right Sort

9B

Objective

- Investigate sorting and searching algorithms and watch them work.

References

Software needed:

1) A web browser (Internet Explorer or Netscape)

2) Applets from the CD-ROM:

   a) Palgo

   b) Searching

   c) Sorting

Textbook reference: Chapter 9, pp. 297–308

Background

Chapter 9, "Abstract Data Types and Algorithms," gets deeper into programming with abstract data types and data structures. Two programming tasks the chapter focuses on are searching and sorting, illustrating various algorithms for both.

Activity

Part 1

Searching and sorting are venerable, respected topics in computer science. In fact, Volume 3 of Donald Knuth's famous series of books, *The Art of Computer Programming*, focuses exclusively on searching and sorting.

You'll be using several applets to explore searching and sorting. The "Palgo" applet provides a complete programming language with arrays (also called lists). Start the applet, select *Example 8–Sorting*, and run the program. Here's a screenshot:

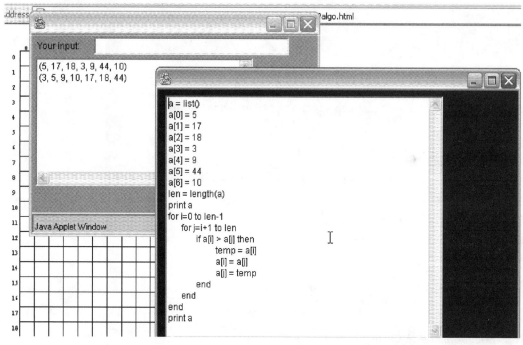

Study the code shown in the screenshot. Can you figure out which of the three sorting algorithms discussed in the textbook was used for this sorting program? Your choices are selection sort (pp. 298–299), bubble sort (pp. 300–201), or quicksort (pp. 301–305).

Notice that the array holding the integers in this program is identified by the variable a. This variable is set to an empty array by the first line:

```
a = list()
```

Then the elements are filled in, one by one:

```
a[0] = 5
```

The length of the array can be discovered by the length function:

```
len = length(a)
```

Unlike some older, better-known languages like C, the programming language in Palgo is fairly easy and forgiving. In C, you have to declare the size of an array when you create it. There are some complex reasons why C requires this but Palgo doesn't—the main reason is that Palgo is *interpreted*, while C is *compiled*. The difference between these two ways of translating high-level code is discussed on pp. 236–238 of the textbook.

Experiment with the Palgo sorting program. As an extra challenge, you might try to encode one of the other sorting or searching algorithms into Palgo language and get it to run (much easier said than done, due to the nature of programming)! If you run Palgo as a standalone application, you can save your programs in a file on disk.

Part 2

Now we will examine the "Sorting" applet. Start your browser and open the "Sorting" applet. The large text area is where you type in a list of numbers. You can load several example datasets by selecting one from the pull-down menu near the bottom of the screen. Then choose a sorting algorithm from the *Sort Choice* pull-down menu in the middle of the window, and finally sort by pressing the *sort* button.

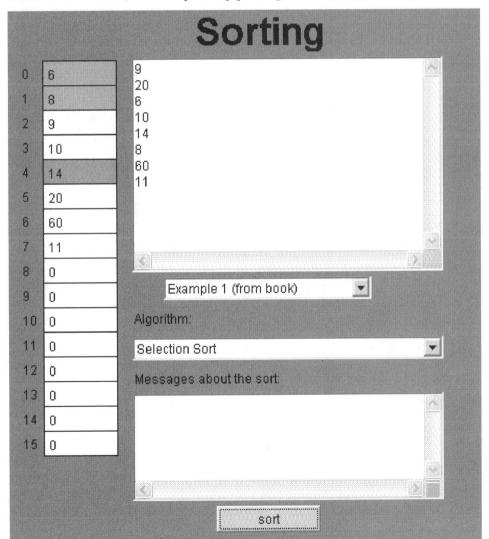

Each of the three algorithms colors the cells slightly differently as they work. The selection sort algorithm colors each cell pink as it examines it. If it decides to swap two cells, it briefly colors those cells red. The gray cells at the top represent the already sorted sublist.

Look at several datasets and use the three different sorting algorithms on them, watching them as they work. The text area above the *sort* button gives the total number of comparisons that the program used while sorting. This can begin to give you a feel for which algorithm is best, and under which conditions it is best.

Of course, there are more than three different sorting algorithms! There is shell sorting, insertion sorting, radix sorting, heap sorting, merge sorting, and others. Even with all these choices, quicksort is perhaps used most often in the "real world." It is found in databases, in the Unix system's sort utility, and in many other places.

Part 3

Closely related to sorting is searching, in which we are trying to find whether a piece of information (such as a number, a character string, or a picture) resides in a collection. Collections are often, but not always, implemented by arrays. Sometimes collections have so many millions of items in them that trees or even more exotic data structures are needed. Trees are discussed on pp. 310–320 of your textbook, and a searching algorithm that is appropriate only for trees is shown in the green box at the bottom of p. 315.

To begin, start the "Search" applet and pull down to select *Example 1*. The applet uses the sequential search algorithm to search for the number 20 in the list. Since 20 is not to be found there, the applet will have to go through the maximum amount of work to find out this fact and report it to us.

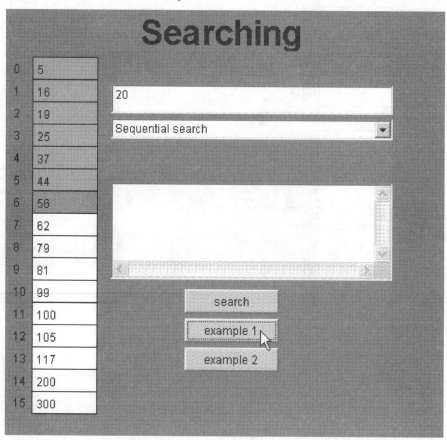

The number of comparisons that it made is reported in the text area above the *search* button.

Type in a number that is found in the list on the left-hand side (such as 56) and click on *search*. This applet intentionally runs slowly so you can watch it at work. In real applications, of course, you would want the fastest program you could get, and animating the search would not be necessary.

Experiment with binary versus sequential search. To use binary search, click on the down-arrow in the menu box in the search applet where it currently says "Sequential Search." What generalizations can you make about their relative speeds? What additional requirements does binary search impose on the dataset?

Exercise 1

Name _____ Date _____

Section _____

1) Start the "Sorting" applet.

2) Make a table in which you can record the performance of the three algorithms on the four different data sets:

	Ex 1	Ex 2	Ex 3	Ex 4
selection				
bubble				
quicksort				

3) Run the applet 12 times and record the numbers it generates in the big white text area.

4) Which algorithm is usually the fastest?

5) Is any one algorithm always faster than the others?

6) Are any two algorithms similar?

7) Did the four datasets cover all the major "cases" you can think of, or are there others? If so, describe them.

Exercise 2

Name _____ Date _____

Section _____

1) Let's experiment with datasets other than those in the examples. Start the "Sorting" applet.

2) In the text area where it says "Your data set goes here," remove the text and type in these numbers. Press return after every number except the last.

        1
        99
        2
        98
        3
        97
        4
        96
        5
        95
        6
        94
        7
        93
        8

3) Are these numbers sorted? Are they arranged randomly? What will the final sorted list look like?

4) Now let's see how our three sorting algorithms perform. Run each of the three algorithms and write down how many comparisons they required to finish the job. (Note: you don't have to retype the numbers in after each sort because the applet refreshes the numbered list on the left with the values you typed into the big text area but does not change the big text area.)

   Selection sort _____

   Bubble sort   _____

   Quicksort   _____

5) Which is the fastest? Does that surprise you?

6) Rerun the quicksort algorithm and write down any patterns you see occurring in the numbered list to the left. For instance, maybe the algorithm quickly moves all of the larger numbers to the top or bottom section.

Exercise 3

Name _____   Date _____

Section _____

1) Now for yet another dataset. Start the "Sorting" applet.

2) In the text area where it says "Your data set goes here," remove the text and type in these numbers. Press return after every number except the last.

```
1
3
8
15
26
45
50
97
92
84
79
72
70
68
51
```

3) Are these numbers sorted? Are they arranged randomly? What will the final sorted list look like?

4) Now let's see how our three sorting algorithms perform. Run each of the three algorithms and write down how many comparisons they required to finish the job.

Selection sort _____

Bubble sort   _____

Quicksort   _____

5) Which is the fastest?

6) Rerun the quicksort algorithm and describe what happens to the number 97.

7) How is quicksort's behavior on this dataset different than its behavior on the previous dataset?

Exercise 4

Name _____ Date _____

Section _____

1) Start the "Searching" applet. The dataset in the numbered list on the left is fixed—you can't change it. However you can select an algorithm and a value to search for.

2) Run all four searches that are in the examples and write down how many comparisons were made:

_____ Example 1: Something in the list (sequential)

_____ Example 2: Something not in the list (sequential)

_____ Example 3: Something in the list (binary)

_____ Example 4: Something not in the list (binary)

3) Select "binary search" as your algorithm and try to find 62. How many tries does it need to find it?

4) Try to find 62 using sequential search. How many tries does it need?

5) Which searching algorithm is clearly superior on this dataset?

6) Is the numbered list on the left sorted? Is this a prerequisite for binary search? Is it a prerequisite for sequential search? (Hint: see p. 306 of your textbook.)

Exercise 5

Name _____   Date _____

Section _____

1) Start the "Searching" applet. Pull down the algorithm menu so that "Binary search" is chosen.

2) This may be a little tedious but there's a reason, so bear with it. For each value in the numbered list to the left, try to find it. Type it into the top text area and click the Search button. Then write down how many tries it required to find it.

   5   _____
   16   _____
   19   _____
   25   _____
   37   _____
   44   _____
   56   _____
   62   _____
   79   _____
   81   _____
   99   _____
   100 _____
   105 _____
   117 _____
   200 _____
   300 _____

3) What is the greatest number of tries needed? _____

   What is the least number needed? _____

   What number of tries appears most frequently in your result list? _____

4) There are 16 values in the list that is searched. Suppose you had 32 values. What do you guess would be the most frequent number of searches? _____

   What if your list had 64 values? _____

Laboratory

10

Operating Systems

Objective

- Watch how the operating system places jobs in memory and schedules jobs.

References

Software needed:

1) A web browser (Internet Explorer or Netscape)

2) Applets from the CD-ROM:

   a) Placement of jobs in memory

   b) Scheduling of jobs

Textbook reference: Chapter 10, pp. 331–337, 347–352

Background

Everything you need to learn is explained in Chapter 10, "Operating Systems."

Activity

Part 1

Operating systems do an amazing variety of tasks, far too many for us to study in detail. The textbook explains several of these in detail, and this lab will show you how to study these and draw your own conclusions about which methods are best.

The first simulation shows how *jobs* that are (programs or sequences of programs submitted by a user) placed in the main memory of a computer by the operating system using single contiguous memory management (textbook p. 339). Start the "Placement of jobs in memory" applet. There is an *Example* button, which places several jobs in memory.

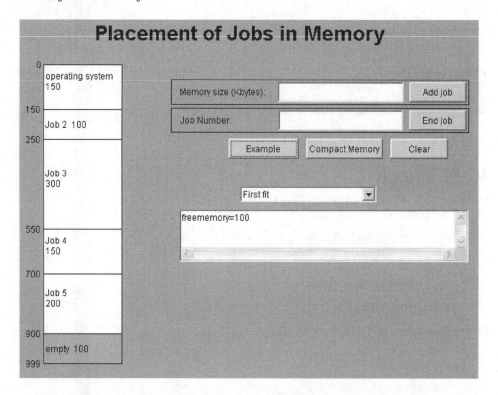

Notice that the operating system always occupies the first 150 kb (kilobytes) of memory, from address 0 up to 149 inclusive.

You can add a new job by typing in a number of kilobytes in the text area near the top and clicking the *Add job* button. Try adding a 200 Kb job. What happens and why?

You can delete a job by typing its job number in the text area next to the *End job* button. Delete Job 2. Notice that the area turns gray to symbolize that this is unused memory. (Of course, the memory itself doesn't change in any way—the power doesn't go off; the bits don't freeze. Jobs are merely an idea in the "mind" of the operating system.)

The power of the simulation comes when several jobs are deleted, leaving "holes" (gray areas) between the jobs. When a new job arrives, it must be placed in memory somewhere. The operating system uses one of three algorithms to find a hole big enough:

1) First fit—the simplest, finds the first hole
2) Best fit—finds the smallest hole
3) Worst fit—finds the largest hole

Sometimes, the total amount of space in all the holes may be enough for the new job, but there is no one hole big enough. In this case, the *Compact Memory* button saves the day—it moves all the jobs to one end and squishes all the free space into one big hole.

Sadly, sometimes there is just not enough memory even after compacting. The operating system then informs the unhappy user to either quit some running programs or give up! Up until recently, home PCs didn't have much memory and messages like this were frequently seen.

This applet allows you to experiment with the three fitting algorithms. Their benefits and drawbacks are explained in the textbook on pp. 341–343.

Part 2

The "Job Scheduling" applet simulates the decisions that an operating system makes when it determines which process gets to use the CPU next. Three algorithms that are discussed in your textbook on pp. 348-350 (First-Come, First Served; Shortest Job Next; Round Robin) are implemented in the applet.

Pull down on the Examples choice menu and select "Example from textbook." A list of jobs is placed in the process list. The first column is the process identifier and the second column of numbers is the list of corresponding service times. These are the time requirements for the process to finish its work. See p. 348 of your textbook.

Select an algorithm and click on Run. If you are impatient, pull down the choice next to "Simulation Speed" and select a faster rate. A log of messages is shown in the big text area on the right, and a Gantt chart is drawn across the bottom of the applet.

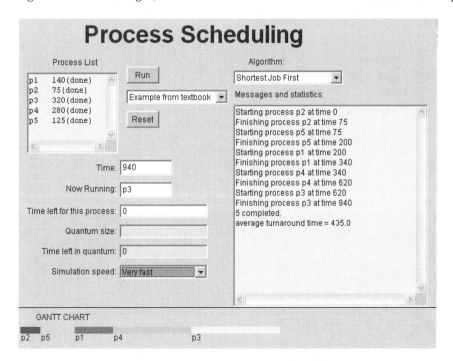

The applet calculates the turnaround time of a process, as described on p. 348 of your textbook. Basically, turnaround time is the service time required by the process plus all the time it spent waiting to obtain the CPU. If there are two processes with service times of 20 and 80, the turnaround time of the first will be 20 for FCFS and SJN, while the turnaround time for the second one will be 100, which is 20 + 80. Thus, the average turnaround time is 120 ÷ 2 = 60.

There are two short example sets of processes and a longer one that appears in the textbook on p. 348. Try all three algorithms on the book example. Notice that when using Round Robin, you can set the quantum size. Its initial value is 50, so that the example on p. 351 will match the applet's result.

Exercise 1

Name _____ Date _____

Section _____

1) Start the "Placement of jobs in memory" applet and click on the *Example* button. Delete jobs 2 and 5. How many holes are there? What is the total amount of free memory? What is the largest job that could be entered without compacting the memory?

2) Try to add a job that is 125 Kb long. What happens?

3) Compact the memory (click on the *Compact* button) and answer Questions 1 and 2 again.

4) Re-start the applet and click on the *Example* button again. (You can re-start the applet by closing and reopening your browser.) Delete jobs 2 and 5 again.

5) Add a job that requires 75 Kb. Where do you expect it to go?

6) Redo Step 4. Select the *Best fit* algorithm from the pull-down menu. Add a 75 Kb job. Where will it go and why? Take a screenshot.

7) Based on your observations of the three algorithms on the example request list, state what kind of request list would make First-Come First-Served (FCFS) take up a lot of time. In other words, what pattern would the numbers in the request list have to show so that FCFS consumes a lot of time.

8) Since the *Compact memory* button is there, why doesn't the operating system always use it when a new job enters? Make a guess as to why frequent compaction is avoided.

Exercise 2

Name _____ Date _____

Section _____

1) Start the "Job Scheduling" applet and click on the *Example* button. Four jobs appear in the job list.

2) Run the program using the *First-Come, First-Served* algorithm. You should get the same answers as shown in the Activity section.

3) Select *Shortest Job first* from the drop-down menu and click on the *Run* button. Does this method have the same total time requirement as the *First-Come, First-Served* algorithm? Note the average time to completion. Is it better than *First-Come, First-Served*? Take a screenshot.

4) Select *Round Robin* from the drop-down menu and click on the *Run* button. Write down the average time to completion. How does it compare to the other two methods? Take a screenshot.

5) Looking at the log of activity, what is fundamentally different about *Round Robin* from the other two job scheduling algorithms? What kind of computing system would likely prefer to use *Round Robin*?

Deliverables

Turn in your hand-written answers. You should also turn in one screenshot from the "Placement of jobs in memory" applet and two screenshots from the "Job Scheduling" applet.

Deeper Investigation

Suppose you have just invented a new job scheduling algorithm and wish to compare its performance to the old standard algorithms. The "Scheduling of jobs" applet can be used as a starting point, but it hardly gives a realistic or easy way to simulate a stream of jobs. Discuss what new features you would put into the applet to enable it to help you in your research. What new buttons and what new functions would you include?

Laboratory

Disk Scheduling

11

Objectives

- Watch how the operating system schedules the reading or writing of disk tracks.

References

Software needed:

1) A web browser (Internet Explorer or Netscape)

2) Applet from the CD-ROM:

   a) Disk Scheduling

Textbook reference: Chapter 11, pp. 377–380

Background

Everything you need to learn is explained in Chapter 11, "File Systems and Directories."

Activity

Lab 10 simulated how the operating system places jobs into memory and schedules jobs. In this lab, we'll look at how the operating system handles scheduling the reading and writing of disk tracks. The "Disk Scheduling" applet presents an imaginary 100-track, single-surface disk drive. That is the tall yellow bar on the left side of the screen. Track 0 is at the top, and track 99 is at the bottom.

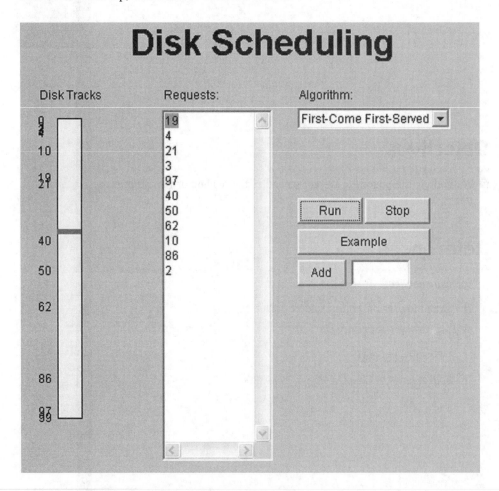

Requests arrive continuously and are kept in a list. Depending on the scheduling algorithm that the operating system uses, a given request may be processed when it is received or much later, depending on where the disk read/write currently is.

For this applet, you'll type in a list of requests. To simplify things, our requests have been stripped down to just which track should be visited next. (In the real world, a request would include information like whether this is a read or a write, which sector to read, what data is to be written, etc.)

Once you have entered some track numbers, click on the *Run* button. You can also preload a list of requested track numbers by pressing *Example.* To start the simulation, press *Run.*

As the simulator is running, you can add new requests by typing in new track numbers into the textfield next to the *Add* button, and then pressing the *Add* button or simply hitting RETURN. In the real world of operating systems, the disk driver is constantly receiving a stream of requests from user programs, which is what you are simulating when you add a new track request.

The read/write head's position is symbolized by a red bar that moves up and down inside the yellow area. As the operating system handles requests, the red bar stops briefly at the current track number, and then removes the request and its number when the request has been completed. Exactly where the red bar moves to next is the subject of the scheduling algorithm.

This applet allows you to experiment with the three scheduling algorithms. Select one of the three from the pull-down menu. The benefits and drawbacks of each algorithm are explained in the textbook.

Exercise 1

Name _____ Date _____

Section _____

1) Start the "Disk Scheduling" applet.

2) Click on the *Example* button, which fills the list with some requests.

3) Select *First-Come, First-Served* from the pull-down menu and click the *Run* button. Time the applet with your watch, or the computer's clock, and write down how many seconds it takes.

4) Select *Shortest Seek Time first* and run the applet again. Measure the time it takes and write it down. Also write down the order of the tracks that are visited. (This is different from the original request list.)

5) Repeat Step 4 after selecting *SCAN Disk (elevator)*.

6) Which algorithm took the least time?

7) Based on your observations of the three algorithms on the example request list, state what kind of request list would make First-Come First-Served (FCFS) take up a lot of time. In other words, what pattern would the numbers in the request list have to follow so that FCFS consumes a lot of time?

Exercise 2

Name _____   Date _____

Section _____

1) Some request lists might cause the disk scheduler to act the same when the three different algorithms are run. Create a request list of five track numbers that will cause all three algorithms to visit the same tracks in the same order.

2) If shortest seek time first starts with the disk head positioned at either 0 or 99, instead of at 50 (in the middle), which algorithm would it resemble: FCFS or SCAN?

   Why?

3) Review Laboratory 9A and Chapter 9, specifically refreshing your memory of stacks and queues. Is the request list of the disk scheduler a stack or a queue?

Exercise 3

Name _____   Date _____

Section _____

1) Start the "Disk Scheduling" applet and type the following numbers into the *Requests* text area:

   8
   20
   35
   80
   10
   90
   5
   87
   26
   94

   These numbers have been chosen so that there are two clusters, one at the lower end of the scale and the other at the upper end.

2) Select the *First-Come, First-Served* algorithm and start. When the disk head has reached 35, type 30 into the "Add" area and press RETURN. This will add a request to seek to track 30 to the list. What happens? Does the disk drive respond to this new request or not?

3) Stop the applet and remove 30 from the end of the list. Choose "Shortest Seek-time first" and rerun the applet. When it consumes 35, type 30 into the add area and press RETURN. Write down what happens. (Warning! You have to be fast because the applet might move into the upper cluster quickly. In that case, just retry.)

4) Stop the applet, remove 30 from the end of the list and choose "SCAN." Run it and when it consumes 35, type 30 again. Write down what happens. Again you must be fast!

5) Which algorithm is least responsive to new requests?

6) Stop the applet, remove 30 from the end of the list, and choose "Shortest seek-time first" and start it. Now try to "trap" the disk head into the lower cluster by typing in disk tracks that are in the lower half of the disk drive, pressing return after each one. You have to be quick, and you may have to try it several times.

7) Redo Step 6, but choose "SCAN" instead. Once again, try to "trap" the disk head into the lower cluster by typing in disk tracks that are in the lower half of the disk drive, pressing return after each one. Were you successful?

8) In real life, disk drives may see a cluster of track requests that could trap it in one section of the disk drive. What implications does this have for programs that requested tracks outside the busy area? (Hint: Computer Scientists have a gruesome term for this phenomenon. It is called starvation. Why do you think they chose this term?)

Deliverables

Turn in your hand-written answers.

Deeper Investigation

The next time you are standing in front of an elevator, waiting for it to arrive, think about the conflicts between fairness and efficiency that the elevator (and operating systems) have to resolve. Though you are undoubtedly the most important person waiting for the elevator, the controlling computer probably isn't aware of this and you won't get priority treatment. What would happen to these scheduling algorithms if some requests did have a higher priority? Do you suppose operating systems ever prioritize disk track requests? Under what circumstances would that be a good idea? What kinds of unforeseen effects might result?

Spreadsheets

Objective

■ Learn some of the basics of a spreadsheet program (like Microsoft Excel).

References

Software needed:

1) A spreadsheet program (preferably Microsoft Excel)

Textbook reference: Chapter 12, pp. 391–399

Background

Chapter 12, "Information Systems," introduces two major types of programs that are used in managing information: spreadsheets and databases. Both of these types are represented by a huge variety of products. Some spreadsheet programs even incorporate simple database functions.

This lab focuses on the spreadsheet program Microsoft Excel, which is widely used and available on both the Macintosh and the Windows platforms. Other programs, such as the spreadsheet program in Microsoft Works, are almost identical to this one. Macintosh office suites such as Appleworks also contain a spreadsheet program, and the formulas are similar. Office suites that exist for Linux, including StarOffice from SUN Microsystems, include a spreadsheet program that will even read and write in the Microsoft Excel file format.

Activity

While this lab uses Microsoft Excel to introduce spreadsheets, most spreadsheets are very similar. If you are using a different program, you may have to make minor adjustments, probably in the names of formulas. Check with your lab instructor for more details.

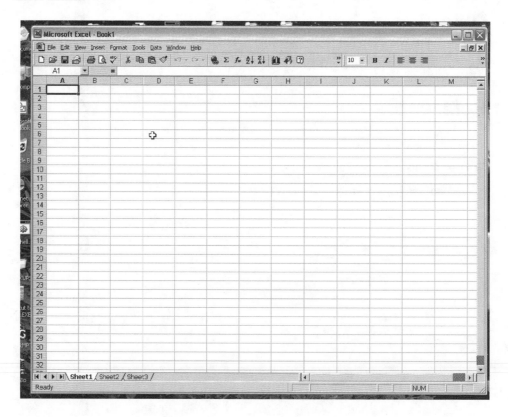

To begin, start Microsoft Excel and a blank worksheet will appear. (The version we are showing here is Excel 2000.)

Your textbook contains all the necessary terminology about cells, formulas, ranges, and functions. Starting in cell A1, type in the data about fictitious pets shown below. Notice that some of the data is numerical and some is textual:

	A	B	C	D	E
1	My Pets				
2		species	birthyear	weight	
3	Sleepy	dog	1992	29	
4	Barky	dog	1989	40	
5	Chewy	lizard	2001	1	
6	Sneaky	cat	1991	12	
7					
8					

Oops! We forgot something. We need to know at a glance how old our pets are so we can buy the right kind of food and take them in for the proper shots. Let's insert a column between birthyear and weight. Click once on the D column header. This highlights the entire column. Then pull down the *Insert* menu and select *Columns*.

Microsoft Excel - Book1

File Edit View Insert Format Tools Data Window Hel

Rows
Columns

D1

	A	B	C	D	E
1	My Pets				
2		species	birthyear	weight	
3	Sleepy	dog	1992	29	
4	Barky	dog	1989	40	
5	Chewy	lizard	2001	1	
6	Sneaky	cat	1991	12	
7					
8					

Don't just type the ages in! They can be calculated by subtracting the animal's birthyear from the current year, 2002. To tell Excel that you are entering a formula that will compute a value, rather than typing the value in directly, start with an equal sign. That doesn't really make a whole lot of sense, but it is the traditional way to enter a formula in most spreadsheets. As shown in the screenshot below, type the formula =2002-c3 into cell D3 of your spreadsheet.

SUM =2002-c3

	A	B	C	D	E
1	My Pets				
2		species	birthyear	age	weight
3	Sleepy	dog	1992	=2002-c3	29
4	Barky	dog	1989		40
5	Chewy	lizard	2001		1
6	Sneaky	cat	1991		12
7					
8					

Press *Return* to finish entering the formula. Excel immediately calculates the result and puts 10 into the D3 cell.

Now we want to enter the same formula for all the animals. But rather than re-typing the formula over and over, let's make Excel do it for us. Put the mouse cursor, which is a large plus sign, on top of D3 and drag it down to D6. All those cells will be highlighted. Excel outlines a highlighted area with a fat black line and then changes the color of the cells to gray.

Next we tell Excel to copy the formula into the first cell of the selected area. Pull down the *Edit* menu and select *Fill*. Since there is a submenu for *Fill*, a right arrow appears. Move the pointer over that arrow to see the next menu, and select *Down*. (Some spreadsheets put the commands *Fill Down* and *Fill Right* in one menu.)

After you complete this operation, you will see the following:

	A	B	C	D	E
1	My Pets				
2		species	birthyear	age	weight
3	Sleepy	dog	1992	10	29
4	Barky	dog	1989	13	40
5	Chewy	lizard	2001	1	1
6	Sneaky	cat	1991	11	12
7					

If you position the mouse cursor over cell D4 (or D5 or D6) and click once, you will see the formula that Excel is using for that cell. In the case of D4, the formula is =2002-C4. But the original formula was =2002-C3. Notice how clever Excel is! It automatically modified the part of the formula that needed to be varied, namely the reference to the animal's birthyear.

So your spreadsheet works pretty well and helps you keep track of your pets' ages. What happens, though, when the ball drops in Times Square on January 1, 2003? Do you have to go in and change all those formulas? Indeed!

However, spreadsheets are enormously clever (well, actually, it's their inventors and programmers who are enormously clever) and they have built into them millions of solutions to pesky problems like this one, our need to keep the year current.

Here's one way: Position your cursor over cell D1 (which was originally empty) and type in the formula =year(now()), as shown next. Press *Return* when you're done. And yes, there are two empty parentheses after the word now, as shown.

SUM	▼	✗ ✓ =	=year(now())	

	A	B	C	D	E
1	My Pets			=year(now())	
2		species	birthyear	age	weight
3	Sleepy	dog	1992	10	29
4	Barky	dog	1989	13	40
5	Chewy	lizard	2001	1	1
6	Sneaky	cat	1991	11	12
7					

What you have done is used the `now()` function, which delivers the current date and time (whenever this cell is recalculated). The `year()` function pulls just the year out of this date and time, so the number 2002 is plopped into cell D1, until you restart Excel on January 1, 2003 and open this spreadsheet, at which point the computer grunts from too much champagne and goes back to bed. (Actually, feeding champagne to your computer is frowned upon!) Okay, what will actually happen is the number 2003 will show up in cell D1.

We still have to make use of this value, so change the formula in cell D3 to the following: `=$D$1-C3`

	A	B	C	D	E
1	My Pets			2002	
2		species	birthyear	age	weight
3	Sleepy	dog	1992	=$D$1-C3	29
4	Barky	dog	1989	13	40
5	Chewy	lizard	2001	1	1
6	Sneaky	cat	1991	11	12
7					

This tells Excel to subtract the birthyear in cell C3 from the year right now, which is kept in cell D1. But what's with those dollar signs? Well, usually cell references used in formulas are *relative* to the cell that contains the formula. That's why the pet's age formula you first entered in cell D3 automatically adjusted itself when you filled the cells beneath it. That original formula you typed in D3, `=2002-C3`, referred to cell C3, just to the left of D3, where Sleepy's birthyear was recorded. When you filled the cells beneath D3, Excel modified the formula in each cell to refer to the appropriate cell to the left, where each pet's birthyear was recorded.

Putting the dollar signs into the formula's cell reference, `=$D$1-C3`, tells Excel that this is an *absolute* cell reference that always refers specifically to cell D1, rather than a relative cell reference that varies depending on the cell in which the formula is located.

Once you've entered the formula `=$D$1-C3` in cell D3, fill the three cells beneath it. The end result will look identical to what you saw before, but the underlying formula makes it more flexible and intelligent, so that you won't have to rewrite your spreadsheet each year.

There are many different spreadsheet functions, far too many to discuss here. Your textbook lists some common ones on p. 397. Virtually every spreadsheet has these functions, but their names vary.

Go to cell D8 and type in

```
=average(D3:D6)
```

	A	B	C	D	E
1	My Pets			2002	
2		species	birthyear	age	weight
3	Sleepy	dog	1992	10	29
4	Barky	dog	1989	13	40
5	Chewy	lizard	2001	1	1
6	Sneaky	cat	1991	11	12
7					
8				=average(d3:d6)	
9					

This computes the average of the cell range D3 through D6. Notice that in Excel a cell range is notated with a colon between two cell addresses, whereas other spreadsheets use two dots (see textbook p. 395). Moreover, some spreadsheets use the function name AVG instead of Average. If you're not using Microsoft Excel, check with your lab instructor or access the online help to see what notation your program uses.

You can control the way numbers, dates, and other material are formatted in cells. Select the cell by clicking on it with the cursor. The cell will become highlighted. Then pull down the *Format* menu and select *Cells....* A new window pops up in which you can determine the number of decimal places and other formats:

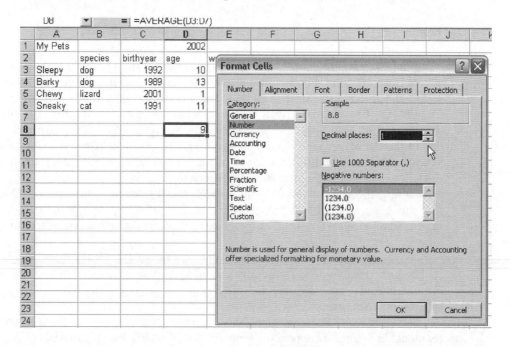

Another commonly used formatting feature is the one that controls the borders and shading of cells. Suppose we want to put a double line underneath the cells that contain the column headings. Highlight cells B2 through E2, pull down the *Format*

menu again, and then click *Cells....* When the tabbed pane appears, click on *Border* to display the border. Click once on the double line in the *Style* area, and then near the bottom of the big white area that says *Text*, as shown below:

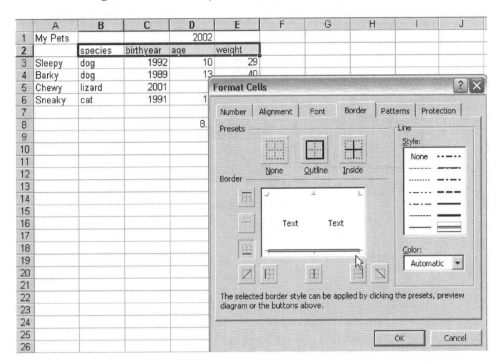

Do this again for the cells containing the pet names, but this time make it a border on the right side of the cells. Next, starting with cell B11, type in the information shown in the screenshot below:

	A	B	C	D	E
1	My Pets			2002	
2		species	birthyear	age	weight
3	Sleepy	dog	1992	10	29
4	Barky	dog	1989	13	40
5	Chewy	lizard	2001	1	1
6	Sneaky	cat	1991	11	12
7					
8				8.8	
9					
10					
11		Animal	Favorite Food		
12		dog	anything		
13		lizard	flies		
14		gorilla	people		
15		cat	tuna		

(Please note: In our hurry to enter some data, any data, into this spreadsheet, we may have gotten a little carried away. There is little in the scientific literature that endorses the notion that gorillas eat humans—in fact, most gorillas seem to find humans distasteful.)

Now we need to put this little table about animal meal preferences into sorted order. For a small list like this it may seem trivial, but sorting is a pretty handy feature when you have large sets of data.

Pull down the *Data* menu and select *Sort....* A new dialog box pops up and we will leave all the defaults as they are; click *OK* to sort.

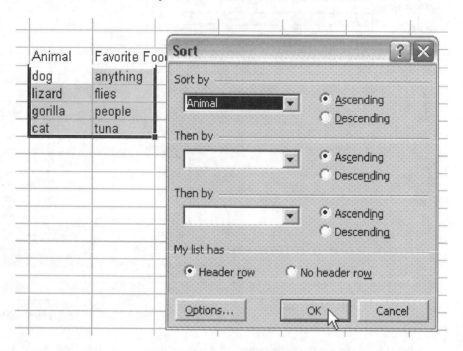

Now let's use that table about animal foods. Assume our dogs, lizard, and cat are all typical animals, and like the favorite food listed for their species. Let's create a new column of pet information in our spreadsheet that will refer to our Favorite Food table to automatically determine what each of our pets prefers to eat. We will use Excel's VLOOKUP formula.

	A	B	C	D	E	F	G	H
1	My Pets			2002				
2		species	birthyear	age	weight			
3	Sleepy	dog	1992	10	29	=vlookup(b3,b12:c15,2)		
4	Barky	dog	1989	13	40			
5	Chewy	lizard	2001	1	1			
6	Sneaky	cat	1991	11	12			
7								
8					8.8			
9								
10								
11		Animal	Favorite Food					
12		cat	tuna					
13		dog	anything					
14		gorilla	people					
15		lizard	flies					

Click on F3 and type in the formula:

```
=vlookup(B3,$B$12:$C$15,2)
```

That's quite a fingerful! What does it all mean? VLOOKUP is a built-in Excel function that looks up items vertically in a table and delivers whatever information is associated with the items. In our example, B3 tells the formula to take the value in cell B3 (dog). Next, $B$12:$C$15 specifies the table spanning the range of cells from B12 to C15 (and, of course, we use the dollar signs again because the table is in an absolute location that stays the same regardless of which cell contains the VLOOKUP formula). The VLOOKUP goes to the specified table and checks to see whether the value contained in cell B3 is also in the first column of the table. Finally, the 2 in the formula tells Excel that if it finds a data match in the first column, it should return with whatever value appears in the second column of the table. VLOOKUP executes a vertical lookup in a table; there is also a horizontal lookup formula called HLOOKUP, which you can investigate on your own.

Here's the final product (with the table left out of the picture):

F3	▼	=	=VLOOKUP(B3,$B$12:$C$15,2)		
	A	B	C	D	E	F
1	My Pets			2002		
2		species	birthyear	age	weight	
3	Sleepy	dog	1992	10	29	anything
4	Barky	dog	1989	13	40	anything
5	Chewy	lizard	2001	1	1	flies
6	Sneaky	cat	1991	11	12	tuna
7						
8				8.8		

The beauty of lookup tables is that if you later find that the favorite food of dogs is "dog chow," you need only change *one thing* in your spreadsheet and it will automatically recalculate all the cells affected by that change. Try it! Go to cell C13, the table cell that says dogs prefer "anything," replace that word with "dog chow," hit *Enter* or *Return* and watch what happens in cells F3 and F4.

Information systems try to avoid redundant information because of the *update problem*. For instance, suppose that you had not used the VLOOKUP function and had just typed the favorite foods in the columns associated with your pets. If you suddenly find that cats hate tuna, but love chicken, you can easily change Sneaky's preference. But if dogs suddenly love dog chow, you have to change two lines. No big deal in this small example, but remember that information in the real world is often amazingly vast and complex. How about a spreadsheet containing a line for every car-owner in the United States? That would stretch into roughly 100 million lines, and you wouldn't want to face the update problem there!

Exercise 1

Name _____   Date _____

Section _____

1) Start Microsoft Excel. You should be looking at a blank worksheet.

2) This exercise will help you compute your grade point average (GPA) for the courses you are taking. In cell A1, type

   `Grade Point Average for Fall 2005 Semester`

   in bold font.

3) Starting in cell A3, type the course identification. This varies from school to school, but usually starts with a departmental abbreviation followed by a course number. For instance, CSC 110 stands for "Computer Science, course #110."

4) In cell B3, type the course name, such as "Introduction to Computing." You should widen column B by dragging on the bar line separating B and C near the top. Here's a screenshot:

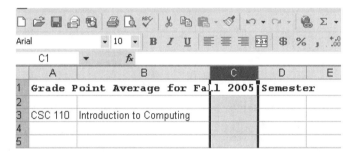

5) In C3, type the number of credit hours for the course, and in D3 the letter grade you either will get, did get, or want to get (depending on where you are in the semester).

6) Now enter some more courses. Many colleges permit students to take five per semester, with labs counting too. If you are on a quarter system or some other schedule, enter your information as appropriate for your school.

7) To turn the letter grades into grade points, you need to convert them to numbers. A lookup table is an ideal way to do this. To the right of your courses, create the lookup table, starting in cell H1. Here's a sample that is appropriate for some schools:

A	4
A-	3.75
B+	3.25
B	3
B-	2.75
C+	2.25
C	2
C-	1.75
D	1
F	0

8) As you can see, the letter grades are on the left and their translated numerical values are on the right. Notice that the letter grades must be sorted in order for VLOOKUP to work.

9) In cell E3, type your lookup function call. Given that the grade table is in cells H1 through I10, you must type:

```
=VLOOKUP(D3,$H$1:$I$10,2,FALSE)
```

although you can use lowercase letters instead. The first argument, D3, specifies that we are going to lookup the value that is in cell D3, which will be a letter grade. The lookup table is given by argument 2, which is a range of cells. The dollar signs fix the range so that it remains exactly cells H1:I10, even if we fill down. The third argument, 2, says that we want to take the value from the 2nd column of the lookup table. And finally the fourth argument, FALSE, tells Excel that we are not looking in a set range in the lookup table, but instead we are trying to find an exact match. This means that if someone gives you a grade of Z or F+, the vlookup function won't find a number for it. If it were a range lookup, Excel would pick a value in the given range.

10) Fill down for the other courses.

11) In cell F3, write a formula that multiplies the number of credit hours by the translated grade. For example, if you entered the grade A− in cell D3, this formula should return 11.1, the value in cell C3 (3) multiplied by the value found in cell E3 (3.7).

12) Fill down for the other courses.

13) Write a function that adds up the column of credit hours. This would look like

```
=SUM(C3:C7)
```

if there were five courses. Adjust the cell range to fit your data.

14) Do a similar sum for the column containing the translated numerical grade values, and another for their multiplied values.

15) Aren't functions fun? Write another one that divides the sum of multiplied values by the sum of credit hours, giving the grade point average. The result should go into C10.

16) Just to make our spreadsheet pretty (and self-explanatory), put some headers in the columns. For instance, in A2, put *Course*. In B2, put *Course name*. Column C gives the credit hours, which you might consider abbreviating at *Cr. Hrs*. Column D is obviously the letter grade. Since the header *Letter Grade* might require the column to be expanded too much, seeing that the contents of the column are very short, let's stand it on end. Click on cell C2 and then click on Format in the menu across the top. When the menu appears, click on Cells...Then click on the Alignment tab and find the orientation section, which looks like half a clock. Click on the top diamond, which is at "12 noon." This means the text will stand on end. Here's what you will see:

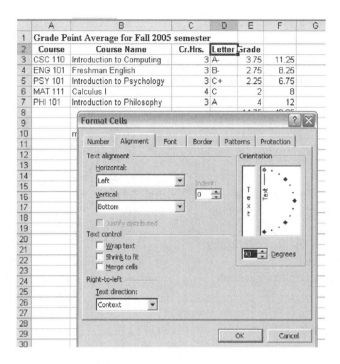

17) Column E is the *Numerical Grade*, and column F is the *Quality Points* for each course. Now center each header cell. To do this quickly, highlight all 6 cells in row 2 and click on the centering icon. (If the centering icon is not on your toolbar, click on Format, select Cells..., Alignment tab, pull down the horizontal menu and select Center.)

18) Unfortunately, by putting the headers in row 2, our spreadsheet looks a little crowded. Let's insert a blank row. Click on the 2 at the edge of row 2, which will highlight the entire row. Then click on Insert in the menu bar. Click on Rows and a new blank row will be inserted.

Wait a minute!!! Won't this screw up our formulas that we so carefully wrote? Actually, no. Excel, like most modern, smart spreadsheets, knows that when you add rows or columns, the formulas have to be adjusted. Click on any formula to put your mind at rest that Excel did adjust them properly.

19) Format the GPA (Grade Point Average) to have 3 places after the decimal point. Format the values in columns E and F to have 2 places after the decimal point.

Here's what your spreadsheet will look like:

	A	B	C	D	E	F
1	**Grade Point Average for Fall 2005 semester**					
2	**Course**	**Course Name**	**Cr.Hrs.**	Letter Grade	Numerical Grade	Quality Points
3	CSC 110	Introduction to Computing	3	A-	3.75	11.25
4	ENG 101	Freshman English	3	B-	2.75	8.25
5	PSY 101	Introduction to Psychology	3	C+	2.25	6.75
6	MAT 111	Calculus I	4	C	2.00	8.00
7	PHI 101	Introduction to Philosophy	3	A	4.00	12.00
8					14.75	46.25
9						
10		my grade point average	3.136			
11						
12						

Exercise 2

Name _____ Date _____

Section _____

1) Start Microsoft Excel or create a new blank worksheet.

2) In this exercise, you will enter some data about the planets of the Solar System. In cell A1, create a title by typing

Planets of Our Solar System

and change its font to Arial 20.

3) In the first column, enter the names of the planets. You might have to expand the width of the column in order for the names to show up properly. You should also create a heading for this column: **Name**. Bold and center it. Here's a snapshot:

Here's the full set of data about the planets

Name	Type	Moons	Mass	Year	Distance
Mercury	rocky	0	0.06	0.241	0.38
Venus	rocky	0	0.82	0.615	0.72
Earth	rocky	1	1	1	1
Mars	rocky	2	0.11	1.88	1.52
Jupiter	gas	63	318	11.86	5.2
Saturn	gas	49	95	29.46	9.54
Uranus	gas	27	14.6	84.01	19.22
Neptune	gas	13	17.2	164.79	30.06
Pluto	rocky	1	0.0017	248.5	39.5

4) In the second column, enter the type of the planet by typing in either **rocky** or **gas**.

5) The third column will contain the number of moons. Enter both the data as well as the header.

6) The fourth column is the mass (amount of material) in each planet, expressed relative to Earth. Many people think of mass as weight, though this isn't correct when there is no gravitational field to pull mass down. Still, mass is the property of material that would exhibit itself in the appropriate place. The Earth's mass is about 5.9736×10^{24} kilograms. That's about 6 septillion kilograms, or 13.2 septillion pounds. Quite huge! Now you can see why astronomers use bigger "units," namely whole planets.

7) The fifth column is the year of the planet, or the time it takes to go around the Sun once. Again, Earth's year is considered to be a unit, which is why it is 1. The way to read this data is that a year on Mars is 1.88 times that of Earth. Since Earth revolves around the Sun in about 365.25 days (yes, that's a fourth of a day), Mars must take 1.88×365.25 or 686.67 days to make one complete trip around good old Sol (our sun).

8) The last column is the distance of the planet from the Sun. Again, Earth is considered 1, because in reality Earth is about 92,750,690 miles from the Sun. (This concept of distance from the Sun is very complicated because the planets vary in their route around the Sun and all orbits are elliptical, or non-circular, which means that sometimes they are farther from the Sun than at other times. Interested students should sign up for Astronomy 101.)

9) In cell C14, put 93. In cell A14, enter "Earth from sun" and in cell D14 "millions of miles." If you type a string of letters in a cell where the column is too narrow, the letters spill over to the next column, unless there is something there already.

10) After you've entered the data, create a thick line under the headers to set them off from the data. Highlight cells A3 to F3. Then click on Format in the main menu in the menu bar. Select Cells...Then click on the Border pane. Click on the thick black line and then click on the bottom of the large white area, which represents the cells whose border you are modifying. Since you selected more than one cell, you will see the word Text twice, indicating two cells.

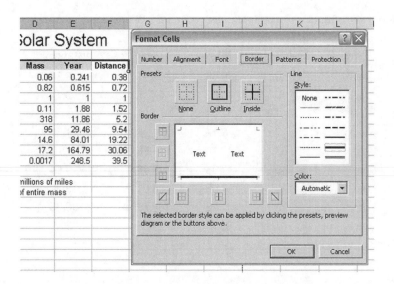

Once you finish entering data, your spreadsheet will look like the following:

	A	B	C	D	E	F	G
1	Planets of Our Solar System						
2							
3	Name	Type	Moons	Mass	Year	Distance	
4	Mercury	rocky	0	0.06	0.241	0.38	
5	Venus	rocky	0	0.82	0.615	0.72	
6	Earth	rocky	1	1	1	1	
7	Mars	rocky	2	0.11	1.88	1.52	
8	Jupiter	gas	63	318	11.86	5.2	
9	Saturn	gas	49	95	29.46	9.54	
10	Uranus	gas	27	14.6	84.01	19.22	
11	Neptune	gas	13	17.2	164.79	30.06	
12	Pluto	rocky	1	0.0017	248.5	39.5	
13							
14	Earth from sun		93	millions of miles			
15	SUN's mass		0.9986	of entire mass			
16							

11) Just entering this much information would be a fair amount of work, but let's practice with some formulas. First, let's show what the mass of each planet is in kilograms. This data should go next to the current mass column, so first we need to insert a new column to the right of D. Click on E to highlight the entire column and then click on Insert in the main menu. Select Columns, which will cause one new column to be added *in front of* the highlighted column.

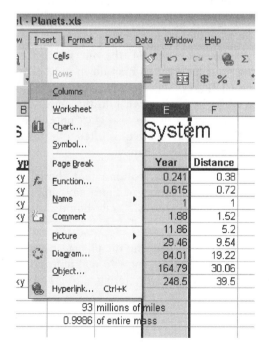

12) In cell E3, put a header **Mass(kg)** to indicate that the data in this column is mass in kilograms. To be perfectly clear, we should back up and change the header for column D to indicate that these mass values are abstract units where Earth = 1. To do this, click on cell D3. Then type **Mass**. Next hold down the ALT key (which is often next to the space bar) and press the ENTER key. This causes a break to occur in the data, putting what follows on the second line. Now type **(Earth=1)** and press ENTER again. This is what it will look like:

	A	B	C	D	E	F	
1	Planets of Our Solar System						
2							
3	Name	Type	Moons	Mass (Earth=1)	Mass(kg)	Year	Dis
4	Mercury	rocky	0	0.06		0.241	
5	Venus	rocky	0	0.82		0.615	
6	Earth	rocky	1	1		1	
7	Mars	rocky	2	0.11		1.88	
8	Jupiter	gas	63	318		11.86	
9	Saturn	gas	49	95		29.46	
10	Uranus	gas	27	14.6		84.01	
11	Neptune	gas	13	17.2		164.79	
12	Pluto	rocky	1	0.0017		248.5	
13							
14	Earth from sun		93	millions of miles			

13) We will put formulas in nine cells, E4 through E12, to express the mass in kilograms. But we won't repeat our work. Instead, we'll put the formula for Mercury into cell E4 and then copy it. In cell E4, type a formula that multiplies the value of D4 by Earth's approximate mass. To avoid typing all those zeroes, use Scientific Notation:

$$=D4*6.0e24$$

Recall that Scientific Notation is a way of expressing extremely large or extremely small numbers. 6.0e24 means 6.0×10^{24}. The letter "e" stands for exponent. Remember that in Excel formulas, the asterisk stands in for the multiplication symbol, partly out of respect for older FORTRAN programmers, but also because X would get confused with the letter X, as in row X.

14) To copy this formula quickly, click once on cell E4, the one we just entered the formula into. Then continue holding your mouse, and drag down until cells E5 to E12 are all highlighted. Hold down the CTRL key and press D, which does a **Fill Down** operation. This copies the formula in the top cell down into the ones below, making adjustments for which rows the cells are in. (You can also click on Edit in the menu bar, click on Fill, and select Down. The keyboard shortcut is often a lot faster!) There is always a **Fill Right** operation, which often comes in handy.

15) Do the same thing for Year, making a new Year column that shows the planet's revolution in Earth days. Use 365.25 for the number of Earth days in an Earth year. The new column's header should say **Year(in days)**. You should also rename the previous column as **Years (Earth=1)**.

16) Finally, we will do the same thing for distance, showing the planet's distance from the Sun in millions of miles by converting the Earth=1 value to real miles by multiplying by 93. However, instead of "hard coding" 93 into every formula, use the Earth distance

that appears in cell C14. But there's a catch here: if you type the following formula and fill down,

=G4*C14

what happens? Something goes wrong. Describe it by looking at the formulas for Venus and Earth.

17) To fix this problem, we need to anchor the C14 cell so it doesn't change in copied formulas. This is discussed in the activity. C14 needs to be changed to an absolute cell reference. Fix the formula for Mercury and fill down again.

Deliverables

Print up your spreadsheet or hand in the file electronically—consult your lab instructor for instructions.

Laboratory

Databases

12B

Objective

∎ Write simple SQL queries using the "Simple SQL" applet.

References

Software needed:

1) A web browser (Internet Explorer or Netscape)

2) Applet from the CD-ROM:

   a) Simple SQL

Textbook reference: Chapter 12, pp. 404–407

Background

Database programs are less standard and generally much more expensive than spreadsheets. Microsoft Access is one of the most popular database programs. Depending upon which bundle of programs you have (called Office Suite), you might have access to Access on your computer. This lab uses an applet called "Simple SQL" to introduce relational databases and SQL (Structured Query Language) queries. Obviously, it is not as big and robust as Microsoft Access—but it has the virtue of being free and portable! If you have access to MySQL, Oracle, or other relational database products, you can experiment with more complicated SQL queries.

Activity

Now that we've worked on spreadsheets, we'll experiment with another application that organizes vast amounts of information: databases. We will focus on SQL queries in a very simple relational database applet. Start the "Simple SQL" applet and click on the *Example Tables* button. This generates two tables, *People* and *CityInfo*, and inserts them into the database. Next, choose *Example 1* from the "example queries" pull-down list:

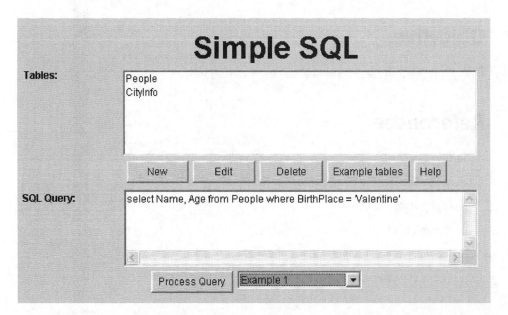

The tables in this database are listed in the upper text box labeled *Tables*. The SQL query appears in the lower box. You can type in your own queries, using select statements similar to those on p. 405 of your textbook, or you can load the examples.

There are some major differences between real SQL and the SQL implemented by this applet. For one thing, this applet supports only a tiny subset of the full SQL language. Also, the applet is case-sensitive, unlike real SQL, in which you can freely mix uppercase and lowercase. The "Simple SQL" applet generally uses lowercase letters, but the names of the fields and the names of the tables, as well as the data inside apostrophes, often contain uppercase letters. For example, the key word **select** is all lowercase, but **Name** and **Age** are the names of two fields from a table named *People*.

Click on *Process Query* and the applet attempts to execute the SQL command in the lower text area. If it is successful, it makes a new table with a name like *result0*, *result1*, etc. These names appear in the *Tables* list in the upper box. You will see a new table, *result0*, added to the *Tables* list.

To view a table, click once on its name and then press the *Edit* button. Do that now with the *result0* table. A new window appears:

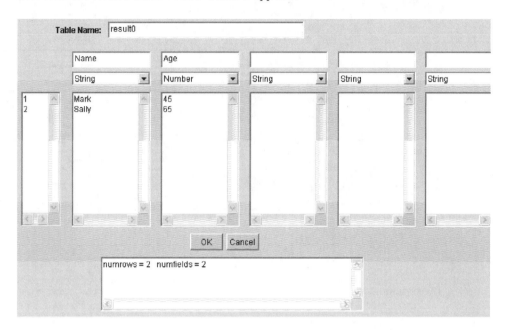

Each field gets its own column, with a name and a type. Only two types are allowed: String and Number. The rows of the table appear across the tops of the columns, and to the left is a list of row numbers. At the bottom is an informational box.

This edit window allows only five fields to be displayed, even though tables in Simple SQL can contain up to eight fields (which is necessary when joining, which we'll talk about in a moment). The textbook explains on p. 406 that there are modification commands in SQL such as *insert*, *update*, and *delete*. Such commands are essential if a program is changing the table, such as a banking program written in COBOL or a medical statistics program written in C++ would do.

However, Simple SQL supports only two commands: *select* and *join*. To change anything in a table, such as the table name, field names, field types, or data in the fields, you must do it in the edit window, then click the *OK* button to save your changes. To add a new field, simply pick a blank column and type in information. Make sure to name your new column of data by typing a name in the blank text field at the top of the column. If Simple SQL does not find a name there, your new field will not be recognized.

To copy a table, select it from the "Tables" list and click the *Edit* button. Rename the table in the edit window and save it by clicking *OK*. To delete a table, click once on its name in the main window and then click the *Delete* button.

When editing, you must be careful if you decide to delete a row. If you delete one row from a particular column, you must delete the same row from the other columns. Otherwise, Simple SQL will line up the rows as they appear in the columns and your data may get "twisted." Also, note that in some circumstances Simple SQL pads out missing rows in some columns with 0. In addition, don't edit the row numbers in the leftmost column. Simple SQL ignores whatever you do there and refreshes the numbers when you re-display the table.

Next, let's *join* for a while. No, this is not carpentry or some collective form of meditation. *Join* is one of those mathematical operations of SQL (textbook p. 406, insert box.) The basis of *join* is the Cartesian product. Select *Example 4* from the pull-down box and click *Process Query*. Look at the resulting table:

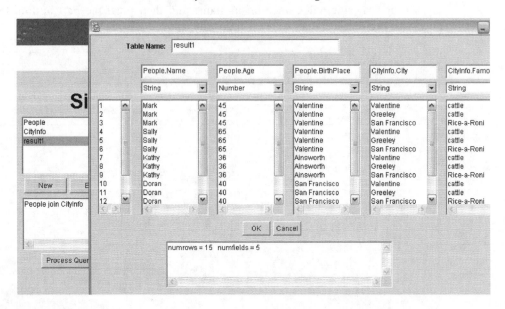

The statement

```
People join CityInfo
```

is a valid SQL statement that takes the Cartesian product. This means that all the fields in both the *People* and the *CityInfo* tables are in the new result, and the rows follow this pattern. For each and every row in *People*, append each row of *CityInfo*. Since there are five rows in *People*, and three rows in *CityInfo*, there will be 15 rows (5x3) in the result. Look at the first three rows of the result: "Mark, 45, Valentine." Notice that this is the same as the first row of *People*. But the first three rows of *CityInfo* are appended to the end, forming three new, unique rows. This is the Cartesian product and the basis of *join*.

Why do tables join? To make room for a large family dinner? No, sorry, tables join so that the information in them can be cross-correlated. In a moment, we will correlate information from both *People* and *CityInfo*. In order to do that, all of the information needs to be temporarily stored in a Cartesian product.

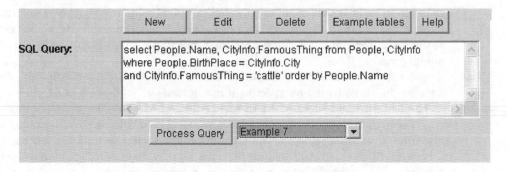

Select *Example 7* from the pull-down menu and take a look at the lengthy SQL query that appears.

Let's figure out what the query will do before we try it. It says that we will select two fields from two tables: *People* and *CityInfo*. (Key words are helpful in deciphering computer statements like this. Look for *select*, *from*, *where*, *and*, and *order by*.) The names of the fields in a joined table are prefixed with the names of the tables from which they came in order to differentiate them, since it is common for tables to use the same field names. You can change the field names by using the edit window.

We aren't going to keep all the rows in the Cartesian product table, though—only those that fit the criteria we specify. We want rows where the BirthPlace field equals the City field, and at the same time those rows where the FamousThing is "cattle." (Of course, these examples, which are quite simplistic and use conjured-up data, are for demonstration purposes only. Valentine, Nebraska, and Greeley, Colorado, are both great places with a lot more going for them than just ranching, as the author knows!)

Notice the *and* keyword that joins the two conditions. You can also join conditions with *or*. Simple SQL also permits the *like* operator for very simple patterns, such as the one on p. 405 of the textbook.

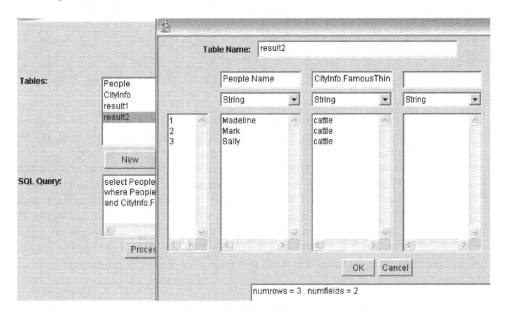

Lastly, the *order* by clause sorts the new table by the indicated field. No changes are made to the existing tables. Only the new one is affected by your query. Let's run the query and see what we get.

Only the cities Valentine and Greeley have "cattle" listed as their FamousThing. Mark and Sally were both born in Valentine, and Madeline was born in Greeley, so this table lists these three people, after sorting by their names.

Let us try one last thing with relational databases. Select *Example 3* from the pull-down menu and click *Process Query*.

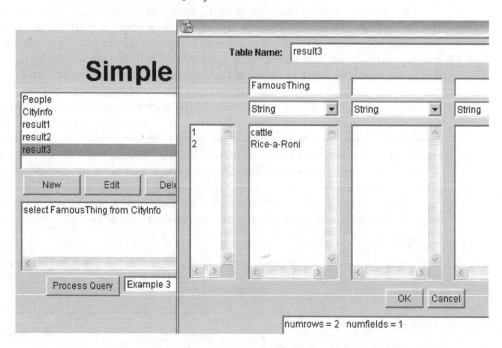

On the face of it, this query is a simple projection of the *CityInfo* table. A projection keeps only the named columns and throws away the rest. It keeps all the rows, however, whereas the `select...where` query throws away some of the rows.

Wait a minute! If you view the original *CityInfo* table (by selecting it and clicking the *Edit* button) you see there were three rows—but in the projection there are only two. What happened? Relational databases typically suppress duplicate rows. That is, they do not permit two rows to be exactly identical in every field. Notice that in the original *CityInfo* table, no two rows were identical. Even though the word "cattle" appears in two rows, the city names were different. When you delete a column, some rows may end up being identical, so databases remove the duplicates.

Tip

Simple SQL can be used as a standalone Java application. If you use it as an application (not as an applet), you can load and save your tables (from the edit window). To run the Java application, navigate to the folder containing the Simple SQL class files and double-click on the **run_application.bat** file.

Exercise 1

Name _____ Date _____

Section _____

1) Start the "Simple SQL" applet.

2) Load the two example tables: *People* and *CityInfo*, by clicking on the "Example Tables" button.

3) Write an SQL query that selects people whose age is greater than 30. Include all fields by specifying `select *`.

4) Now print out only the names of these people. (This is a `select` statement that looks like *Example 3*.)

5) Edit the result so the window pops up, displaying the result table, and take a screenshot.

Exercise 2

Name _____ Date _____

Section _____

1) Start the "Simple SQL" applet.

2) Load the two example tables: *People* and *CityInfo*.

3) Edit the *CityInfo* table and add a new field called Population. Its type is Number. Fill in the following information: San Francisco has about 800,000 people, Valentine 2,000, and Greeley 60,000.

4) Write an SQL query that prints out the cities where cattle is the FamousThing. We don't want to see any other field except the city name.

5) Take a screenshot of the resulting table.

6) Now write an SQL query that prints out the famous thing of "big cities," where big means the population is over 100,000.

7) Take a screenshot of the resulting table.

Exercise 3

Name _____ Date _____

Section _____

1) Keep using the "Simple SQL" applet. You will need the modified *CityInfo* table that has the population from Exercise 2.

2) Write an SQL query that prints out the names of the people in the *People* table alongside the population of the city in which they were born. (For help in writing this, look at *Example 7* in the applet.) Your result may be sorted or unsorted.

3) Take a screenshot of the main window so that your SQL query appears.

Exercise 4

Name _____   Date _____

Section _____

1) Start the "Simple SQL" applet and load the two example tables: *People* and *CityInfo*.

2) Edit the CityInfo table and add a row for Ainsworth. Its famous thing is "corn." (You do not need to type in a row number since the applet will fill this in when you save it.)

3) Add a new field called *State*. Its type is String. Fill in the following information: Valentine and Ainsworth are in Nebraska; Greeley is in Colorado, and San Francisco is in California.

4) Take a screenshot. Save your changes by clicking on the OK button.

5) Now we will make an entirely new table. Back at the main Simple SQL window, click on New. An edit window will pop open with an empty table named *newtable*. Change the name to *StateInfo*.

6) Set up three fields:

   Name: Name of the state

   Capital: Name of the capital city

   Population: Total population of the state

   Bird: The state bird

   Can you guess the proper types of each of these?

7) Put the right data into each field. You could look up this data on www.wikipedia.com, but here it is for your convenience:

California	Sacramento	33,871,000	California Quail
Nebraska	Lincoln	1,711,000	Meadowlark
Colorado	Denver	4,301,000	Lark Bunting

   (The applet will permit you to type commas into your numbers, which is very humane. Many computer applications and programming languages are more persnickety.)

8) Take a snapshot of the table and click OK to save your changes to *StateInfo*.

9) Now we are going to link three tables at once, which is definitely not for the faint of heart. We do this in order to answer the following question:

   What are the names of the state birds for each of the people in our People table?

   See if you can answer this "by hand" first without writing SQL. As you struggle to find the people's birthplace, and what state those birthplaces are in, and what the state bird of the state that those birthplaces are in is...Whew! Gets complicated! This is why computers are still not able to understand human language—there's so much to know and so much logic to use when you chain facts together.

10) Now comes the computer part: write an SQL query that answers this question. Once you get the SQL query correct, take a snapshot of your screen. (Hints in next numbered item...)

11) There are several ways to tackle this. You might first join *People* and *CityInfo*, which is Example 4, and then join the resulting table with *StateInfo*. However, our applet only permits five columns per table, so you will have to project out unnecessary columns, like the people's ages.

12) A better way is to write one SQL statement, like Example 7, that implicitly joins the tables. Unfortunately, Simple SQL requires that no more than two tables appear in a single SELECT statement, a restriction that grown-up databases like Oracle and MySQL do not share. But you can write two SQL statements to do the joins. You will have to write one SQL query statement and process that, take a snapshot, and then write a second SQL query statement and process that, taking a second snapshot.

Deliverables

Turn in your screenshot showing your program after it finishes running, and your screenshot showing the edit window with your program in it.

If you are running Simple SQL as a standalone Java application, save your tables and then print them out. Use a word processor or a text application (like Notepad or SimpleText) to print out the file. Your instructor may ask you to hand in the file electronically, too. Consult the instructor for details on how to do this.

Deeper Investigation

Databases get a bad rap as being boring, sort of like cost accounting for business majors. However, there are a lot of fascinating issues, and it can be great fun writing tricky queries to get the computer to do your bidding, not unlike programming.

One thing that many databases require you to identify is a *key*, which is one of the fields, or a combination of the fields, that uniquely identifies the rows of a table. Can you find keys in both the *People* and *CityInfo* tables? What kind of keys would be good to use in a large database of the general population? Which fields would not be keys, because the information is duplicated?

Lastly, let's think about how human language interacts with SQL. Interestingly, SQL was originally named SEQUEL, for "Structured English Query Language," because its inventors at IBM wanted people to think that they could almost talk to the computer in a natural way.

There are several things that make translating ordinary language into query language difficult: ambiguity of words, changes in syntax, and different vocabulary. Think of several English words that are obvious synonyms. Then try writing one of the Example queries in more or less normal English, something you could give to a brother or sister who doesn't know SQL, but that would tell them what to do with the data. Lastly, take an English description of some data you would like and see if you can cast that into an SQL query. There are some programs that attempt to do this, but they are far from complete or foolproof.

Many spreadsheets act as databases. For example, Excel allows you to make simple queries involving selection. A deeper question is: Why do we need separate applications if the boundaries are so blurry that spreadsheets end up acting like databases, and databases incorporate spreadsheet functionality?

Laboratory

Artificial Intelligence

13

Objective

- Learn how semantic networks and rule-based natural language systems can simulate intelligent behavior.

References

Software needed:

1) A web browser (Internet Explorer or Netscape)

2) Applets from the CD-ROM:

   a) Semantic networks

   b) Eliza therapist

Textbook reference: Chapter 13, pp. 417–424, 433–437

Background

Artificial Intelligence is discussed in Chapter 13 of your textbook.

Activity

Part 1

Knowledge is an essential part of acting intelligently, as is a method for using that knowledge. Computers running AI programs use information to make decisions, filter inputs, and generate new knowledge. The structure of information inside the computer's memory is called a knowledge representation technique. Semantic networks are one kind of knowledge representation technique. They are often depicted as graphs of linked nodes (textbook p. 422). However, the graph can be represented textually by statements, and of course computers are much more comfortable with text than with pictures.

The "Semantic networks" applet allows you to enter rules in English statements and then ask a question called a *query*. Applying the rules using a process known as deduction, the applet tries to answer the query. If it can positively answer the question, the applet says, "This is true." If it can't, it says the statement is false or cannot be answered. Some logical deduction systems, such as the Prolog language, use the closed world assumption, meaning that all information that is true is included in the rule base, anything that is not in the rule base, is false. Other AI systems do not make such a grand assumption, and merely state that they cannot prove a statement is true if it's not in the rule base. The statement might be false, or the rule base might be incomplete.

Start the "Semantic networks" applet and click on the *Example* button. Then rev up the logic inference engine by clicking on *Is this true?* Here's what you will see:

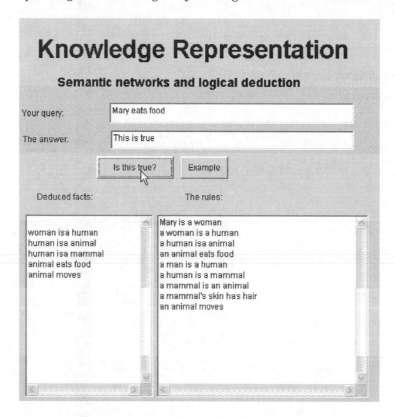

Experiment with some other queries, such as `a woman eats food` or `a man is an animal`. The applet requires that you use no punctuation or capital letters.

Type in the query `a woman is a man`. What does the applet say? If we type `Mary has blood`, we also get "This is false or can't be answered." While we know this statement is true, our very small rule base doesn't cover that topic, so deduction is impossible.

Obviously, it would take a very large rule base to create a robust, "real world" logical deduction system. Just how large the rule base would have to be is a hotly debated issue in AI. Computer scientist Doug Lenat has been building a gigantic system named CYC for over 10 years. (CYC is pronounced "sike" and is short for enCYClopedia.) He believes that if about 10 million common sense facts are stored in CYC, it can begin to function like a human. Perhaps you'd like to try typing 10 million facts into the applet to see if it's able to function like a human.

As you're typing in your 10 million rules, be aware that the applet is very limited in terms of the kinds of phrases it can process (we won't use the loaded word *understand* anymore). Here are the patterns the applet processes:

```
noun isa noun
noun verb
noun verb object
noun's noun verb object
```

The only *keyword* (meaning a word that must appear exactly as it is, without substitutions) is `isa`. English words can be substituted for all the others. The 's that is tagged onto the end of the first noun is optional.

You might be wondering about this key word `isa`, since you can see that the rules contain regular English statements like `Mary is a woman`. The reason you can use regular English in the rules is because of the clever way the applet processes rules and queries. First, it combs through the rules and queries, replacing phrases like `is a` and `is an` with our keyword `isa`, as you can see in the *Deduced facts* column. Also, notice that articles such as `a`, `an`, and `the` are totally eliminated. This kind of pre-processing is very common in computer systems because it simplifies the programmer's task.

The logical deduction system inside this applet matches patterns. If a query matches a rule exactly, it is true. If not, the applet tries to replace the first noun with a second one that appears in an `isa` rule. For instance, we know that the statements `woman isa human` and `human isa animal` and `animal eats food` are all true. By making two replacements, we find out that `woman eats food`. Since `Mary isa woman`, we can safely conclude that `Mary eats food`. The same happens for possessive nouns; they can also be replaced by their *superclasses*. (`human` is a superclass of `woman`, and `animal` is a superclass of `human`.)

Tip

"Semantic networks" can be used as a standalone Java application. If you use it as an application (not as an applet), you can load and save your rules. To run the Java application, navigate to the folder containing the Semantic networks class files and double-click on the **run_application.bat** file.

Part 2

One of the classic, early AI programs is ELIZA, written by Joseph Weizenbaum in 1963. An example of a famous ELIZA conversation with a human is given on p. 438 of the textbook. ELIZA appears to be a therapist who responds to a patient's statements by cleverly rewording them and turning them into questions. Though ELIZA's method sounds pretty simple, and though no one could persuasively argue that the computer is really thinking when it is running ELIZA, the program's effect on people was surprisingly powerful. In fact, Dr. Weizenbaum, shocked by people's reactions and fearing the potential for misuse of artificial intelligence, turned against the field!

To begin, start the "ELIZA therapist" applet and type a question or statement into the top text area, pressing *Return* when you're done. ELIZA responds in the text area below. A running transcript of your inputs and the computer's responses is kept in the larger area below that. After you type for a while, click on the *Show rules* button.

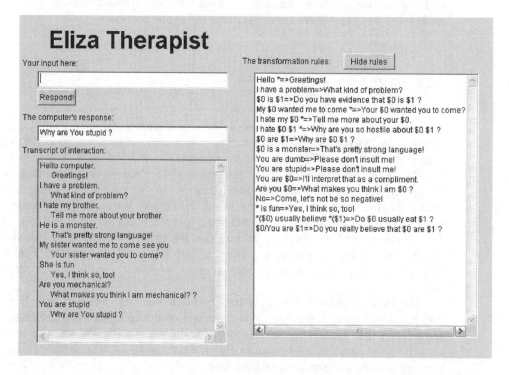

The original Eliza used only a few simple rules. Eliza turned the client's statement into a question merely by appending a question mark to the statement and switching the pronouns, as shown below:

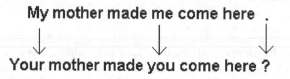

Eliza didn't even use the complicated English question construct "Did your mother make you come here?" This is more difficult because the verb has to be changed and a form of the verb "to do" has to be inserted.

Our version of Eliza uses a different approach. Instead of one or two simple transformation rules, the applet allows the user to enter any number of rules. Eliza then tries to match the input statements with the rules, mixing up the order by starting at a random spot in the list each time.

The rules have the form

```
pattern=>response
```

Inside both the pattern and the response, variables can appear. They are marked with a question mark and are followed by the numbers 0, 1, 2, etc. For example:

```
My $0 made me come here *=>Why did your
                        $0 make you come here?
```

In this pattern, $0 is matched against a single word that appears between the words My and made. The asterisk at the end of the pattern means none, a few, or many words may appear here. They are ignored. The words that must match are My, made, me, come, and here, in that order, with a word between My and made, symbolized by $0.

If Eliza can't find a rule that matches the statement, it moves on to the next rule. If no rules match any of the statements, Eliza picks a standard response such as "Let's move on" or "Tell me more."

If you want to match one or more words, surround the variable with an asterisk and parentheses, as in the following rule:

```
*($0)=>$0 ?
```

This rule merely spits back the statement as a question, although it doesn't do pronoun switching like the original Eliza. You can see pronoun switching in some of the other rules.

Another thing that you can put in a rule is to forbid the matching of some words, as in the following rule:

```
$0/You are $1=>Do you really believe
that $0 are $1 ?
```

This rule tries to match a sentence that has "are" as the second word, but the first word *cannot* be You. Also, as shown in the rule above, if your rule ends with a variable followed by punctuation, leave a space between the variable and the punctuation mark.

Unfortunately, this Eliza applet has many limitations. Some of the purely mechanical ones include the inability to recognize uppercase and lowercase words as essentially the same word. It also doesn't know about English grammar rules, such as the rule that only plural nouns may precede the verb are. Thus, Water are wet would be accepted by the above rule—which is clearly wrong!

Eliza's use of key words when matching rules to client inputs can result in inept responses. A classic example is:

Client: Necessity is the mother of invention.
Eliza: Tell me more about your mother.

Eliza knows nothing about metaphors, hyperbole, or similes. In short, Eliza flunked high school English!

In addition, of course, Eliza cannot be said to *understand* the client's input. Thus, it converses without thinking, as happens far too often at cocktail parties and political rallies. There are other AI systems that actually attempt to tease out the meanings of the words and phrases, but they are still largely experimental. Natural language understanding is a *long* way off from the chatty computers on the TV series *Star Trek*!

Tip

Eliza can be used as a standalone Java application. If you use it as an application (not as an applet), you can load and save the transformation rules. To run the Java application, navigate to the folder containing the Eliza class files and double-click on the **run_application.bat** file.

Exercise 1

Name _____ Date _____

Section _____

1) Start the "Semantic networks" applet.

2) Add a new isa rule to the rule base. This rule may extend the human/animal categories or do something entirely different.

3) Add a new rule that uses a verb other than is and mentions your new category.

4) Add a new rule that gives a characteristic of your new category. This rule puts your new category in front, in the form of a possessive noun.

5) Type in one query that should evaluate to "true." Take a screenshot.

6) Type in another query that should evaluate to "false." Take a screenshot.

7) Type in

John's skin has hair

and press the button "is this true?" Explain the applet's answer.

8) If the applet says this is false, what rule could you add to the rule box so that it would deduce it as true?

Exercise 2

Name _____ Date _____

Section _____

1) Start the "Eliza therapist" applet.

2) Click on *Show rules.*

3) Type in a rule that turns the client's statements:

   My _____ is ruined

   into:

   Are you sure your _____ is ruined

4) Test out your new rule by pretending to be the client.

5) Add a new rule that turns the client's statements:

   I have a _____ for a pet

   into:

   It must be interesting to have a _____

   The first blank, however, *cannot* be the word "cat."

6) Test this new rule. Take a screenshot, showing the rules and the above two statements, along with Eliza's responses.

7) Type in a statement that makes Eliza come up with a grammatically incorrect response. Take in a screenshot.

8) Type in a statement that makes Eliza come up with a nonsensical response, similar to the "mother of invention" non sequitur on page 205 of this manual. Take a screen shot.

Deliverables

Turn in two screenshots from the "Semantic networks" applet, clearly showing your three new rules, your queries, and the response. Also, turn in two screenshots from Eliza.

If you are running "Semantic networks" or Eliza as standalone Java applications, save your rules files. Your instructor may want you to hand them in. Consult the instructor for details on how to do this.

Deeper Investigation

Think back to the statement `a woman is a man`, which the "Semantic networks" applet claimed was false or unanswerable. We know this statement to be false because the categories `woman` and `man` are mutually exclusive. The power of our logic machine could be vastly increased if we added some *metarules*, or rules about rules. In this case, a thing can't belong to two mutually exclusive categories. That's the metarule. Then we would have to tell the machine that `woman` and `man` are mutually exclusive. The great thing about this approach is that we can type in a bunch of mutually exclusive categories, and the metarule would instantiate the actual rules that make the inferences. For example, a metarule that states `woman` and `man` are mutually exclusive categories of "human" would automatically create all these rules.

```
woman isa human
man isa human
woman is not a man
man is not a woman
```

Can you think of other mutually exclusive categories? When does the line get fuzzy? Is the real world essentially nice and clean, or essentially messy? Also, can you think of other useful metarules? Finally, try to imagine how to build a system that could learn new rules on its own instead of relying on a human to type in millions of rules.

Laboratory

Simulating Life & Heat

Objective

∙∙

■ Experiment with two simulation applets: "Game of Life" and "Heat transfer."

References

∙∙

Software needed:

1) A web browser (Internet Explorer or Netscape)

2) Applets from the CD-ROM:

   a) Game of Life

   b) Heat transfer

Textbook reference: Chapter 14, pp. 451–455, 458–465

Background

The concepts of simulation and modeling are presented in Chapter 14, "Simulation and Other Applications."

Activity

Part 1

Life was invented around 1970 by John Conway. It is an example of a *cellular automaton*, a simple "machine" whose parts are very rudimentary but whose overall behavior is surprisingly complex. The "parts" of the Life machine are the squares, and a few simple rules govern what these parts do.

In Life, each square that is black is said to be "alive," and each white square is "dead." The board of squares is shown at a certain time *t*. The machine decides whether each square will be alive or dead at time *t+1* using the following rules:

1) If a square has exactly three neighbors that are alive, it will be alive in the next time period.
2) If a square is alive and has one or no alive neighbors, it dies of loneliness.
3) If a square is alive and has four or more neighbors, it dies of overcrowding.
4) If a square has two neighbors, it is unchanged.
5) The squares at the edge do not change.

A little bit of terminology is necessary. A *neighbor* of a square is one whose row number or column number differs from the square's by just 1. This means the squares directly above, below, to the left, and to the right of a square are that square's neighbors, as are the squares on the diagonals. In the following picture, the gray cells are neighbors of the black square:

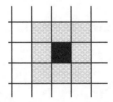

Start the "Game of Life" applet. Click on the *Example* button, which inserts a pattern of black squares on the grid, then click on *Play Game* to watch it go. Eventually this game stabilizes: the black square "life forms" will either cease moving and come to a stop, or reach a point where they continue moving in a consistent and unchanging pattern, or disappear completely. Click on the *Stop* button to end the game.

The Game of Life

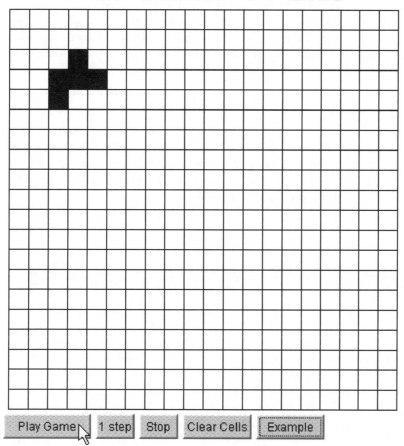

Now it's your turn to become master of this tiny universe. Clear the cells and click on several squares. If the square is white, it becomes black. If the square is black, clicking on it turns it white. Make a pattern and play the game.

You can either let the game run continuously by clicking once on *Play Game,* or you can advance the simulation one step at a time by clicking on *1 step.* See if you can follow the rules for a few cells by advancing only one step after trying to predict the results.

Various computer scientists have been fascinated by the Game of Life throughout the years. Steven Levy, in his 1984 book *Hackers,* tells about Bill Gosper and others at the MIT Artificial Intelligence lab who programmed Life on PDP-6 computers and then became obsessed with trying to predict what patterns would emerge. You can have some fun, too, (even become obsessed if you'd like) by experimenting with different patterns and categorizing their behaviors.

The pattern that the *Example* button inserts generates some interesting sub-patterns. Some of these patterns are very stable, such as four black squares that form a 2x2 square. It just sits there and does nothing (unless some neighbors come creeping up on it). Another stable pattern is a line of three squares. It seems to rotate forever. One pattern that also shows up is the glider, which moves across the screen. Gosper and his friends tried to create all kinds of gliders and other patterns that perpetuated themselves.

The Game of Life fits into several subfields of computer science, including simulation and artificial intelligence. It can be considered an example of simulation because Life models a simple universe and shows how to *discretize* (i.e., break into chunks) time and space. The link with AI is historical; many early AI researchers were fascinated by it and wondered what it meant. On a deeper level, Life is an example of how a few simple rules generate *emergent* behavior that is complex and unpredictable. Some AI researchers believe this is how plants, animals, humans, and societies derive their complexity: from simpler subsystems that interact in surprisingly complicated ways.

Tip

Game of Life can be used as a standalone Java application. If you use it as an application (not as an applet), you can load and save your pictures. To run the Java application, navigate to the folder containing the Game of Life class files and double-click on the **run_application.bat** file.

Part 2

The conduction of heat through a solid material is illustrated by the "Heat transfer" applet. It is similar to the Game of Life in that time and space are discretized. Simple rules are applied to the space chunks, called cells, in order to generate the values of the characteristic variables of these cells in the next time frame.

In the "Heat transfer" applet, the only characteristic value we are interested in is the temperature of the cell. The rule is quite simple: the temperature of a square in the next time step will be the weighted average of the temperature of that square in the current time step and the four direct neighbors' temperatures. This is called a five-point update stencil. (The Game of Life used an eight-point update stencil because it excluded the square in the middle but included the four diagonal neighbors.)

If you really want to impress your friends, show them the following equation, which governs the "Heat transfer" applet:

$$T_{i,j}^{(t+1)} = \frac{T_{i-1,j}^{(t)} + T_{i,j-1}^{(t)} + T_{i+1,j}^{(t)} + T_{i,j+1}^{(t)} + 4*T_{i,j}^{(t)}}{8}$$

The subscripts are the row and column numbers. The superscripts in parentheses are the times. This merely says that the temperature of cell *i,j* at the next time step is the average of itself and its neighbors at the present time step. However, the cell itself is multiplied by 4, because its temperature counts for more than its neighbors. This is one parameter of the simulation and has the effect of *dampening*, or slowing down, the effects of a cell's neighbors on its new values.

Start the "Heat transfer" applet and click on *Example 1*. A pattern of colored squares appears, with a legend to the right indicating the temperature range (from 0 to 1.0). Red indicates the hottest temperature and black the coldest. This entire array of squares is assumed to be surrounded by an infinite number of always-cold squares. Click on *Run* to watch the simulation:

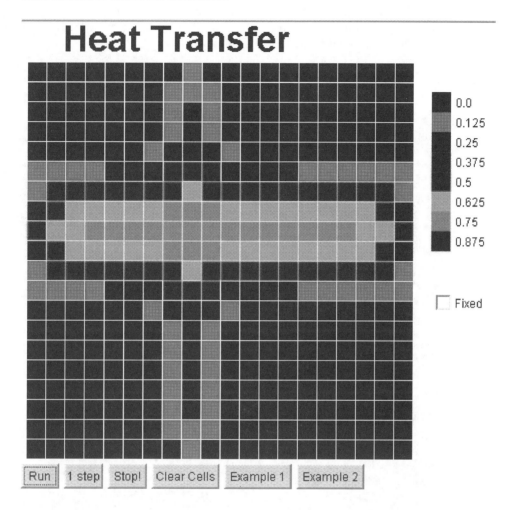

In this example, the entire grid of cells cools off to 0 eventually, making it completely black. (Do you agree with many leading physicists that this is the fate of our universe, although it probably won't happen for another 10^{100} years?)

Now stop the simulation and click on *Example 2*. This creates a small rectangle of red-hot cells near the bottom of the grid, and also fixes their values. You can tell when the values are fixed because a tiny white square appears in the lower right corner. Run the simulation for a while and watch the flame pattern emerge. Think of the red rectangle as a heating element or a burning wick:

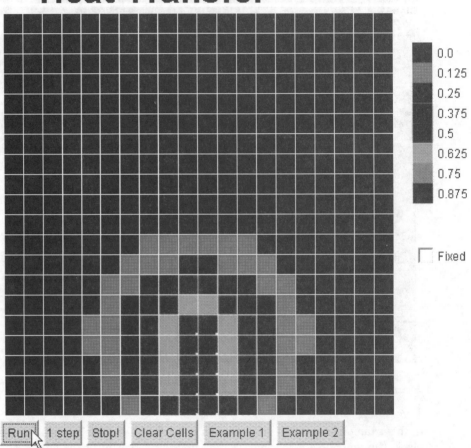

You can create your own pattern by clicking *Stop!*, then *Clear Cells*, and then clicking your mouse on the grid. To set the current temperature, click on one of the legend squares to the right, then click on a square in the grid. If the *Fixed* box is checked, the temperature that you set for a square in the grid will be fixed and the simulation will not change it. A square can be changed to not fixed by unchecking the *Fixed* box, then clicking on the cell again. The little white square in the lower right corner tells you which cells are fixed.

Exercise 1

Name _____ Date _____

Section _____

One of the amazing things about the Game of Life is how utterly unpredictable it is. Classical science wants to make predictions about objects based on the characteristics of the objects. But two very similar objects in the Game of Life universe can cause wildly different behavior. Chaos theory grew out of this situation.

An object in the Game of Life is a pattern of black cells on the grid. In this lab we will investigate a series of similar objects and try to categorize their behaviors.

1) Start the "Game of Life" applet.

2) Draw a series of vertical lines in the middle of the screen of varying lengths. Start out with a single box. Click on "Play Game" to start the simulation. Let it run for a while and record the final configuration of the black cells in the table below and how many simulation steps it took to reach that configuration. Use the following codes for configurations:

D   disappear   all black cells vanish, the grid is all clear

O   oscillating   the grid changes between two different arrangements of cells forever

S   stable   the image is frozen into one arrangment

C   changing   the image keeps changing for a long time

As an example, a line of length 1 disappears very quickly. A line of length 3 oscillates between a horizontal and vertical line. A square of four black cells is stable.

For a second example, here's a vertical line of 5 black cells and what the screen looks like after 53 simulation steps:

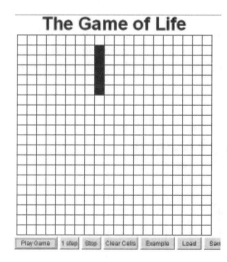
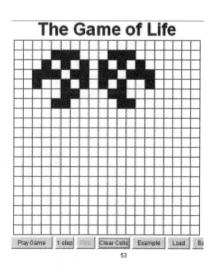

This pattern might be called C for changing. But let it run for longer and see if the screen disappears, or if the pattern freezes, or if it oscillates.

Make sure that the ends of your lines are not border cells, and that your line is in the middle of the screen. Since slightly different rules apply to border cells, the behavior of your line will change if it is up against an edge of the grid.

Here's the table to fill out:

Line length	ending config.	time to reach	notes
1	blank	1	disappears almost completely
2			
3			
4			
5			
6			
7			
8			
9			
10			
11			
12			
13			
14			

3) Are there any patterns in your data? Can you draw any conclusions?

4) Repeat the same experiment, only draw horizontal lines along the top of the grid. Once again, the variety of patterns and unpredictability is fascinating. Here is a screenshot of a 14-cell line, after a number of simulation steps. What the picture can't show is that part of the diagram oscillates.

The Game of Life

Line length	ending config.	time to reach	notes
2	_____	_____	
3	_____	_____	
4	_____	_____	
5	_____	_____	
6	_____	_____	
7	_____	_____	
8	_____	_____	
9	_____	_____	
10	_____	_____	
11	_____	_____	
12	_____	_____	
13	_____	_____	
14	_____	_____	

Exercise 2

Name _____ Date _____

Section _____

1) Start the "Game of Life" applet.

2) Create the following pattern on screen, placed in exactly the grid cells shown.

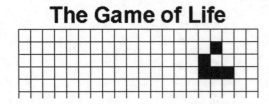

3) Is this a glider? Define "glider."

4) When does the glider stop and why?

5) Experiment with this pattern of five cells and see if every rotation is also a glider. For example, flip the pattern horizontally:

The Game of Life

6) Flip the pattern vertically and see if that is also a glider.

7) Flip the pattern vertically and horizontally and see if that is a glider, too.

Exercise 3

Name _____ Date _____

Section _____

1) Start the "Game of Life" applet.

2) Create the following pattern on screen, placed in exactly the grid cells shown. Notice that it is the same glider pattern, but now it is up against the edge.

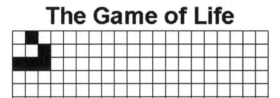

3) Describe the behavior of this pattern. Is it a glider? Does it end? Does it oscillate?

4) Many patterns oscillate. A vertical line of three black cells oscillates. How many simulation steps occur before the original pattern repeats?

vertical line of 3 cells _____

pattern above _____

horizontal line of 7 cells
along the top _____

5) What is the difference between an oscillator and a glider?

Exercise 4

Name _____ Date _____

Section _____

1) Start the "Heat transfer" applet.

2) Check "Fixed" on the right edge of the black grid. Click on the red box in the legend. Then click on one cell right in the center of the black grid.

3) Start the simulation by clicking on the "Run" button. Run for about 30 seconds and take a screenshot.

4) Describe the pattern of colors that you see.

5) Does this pattern fit your intuition of what would happen if you put a red hot coal in the middle of a cold room?

6) List one way that the simulation doesn't quite mimic what really happens to a red hot coal in a cold room.

7) Let the applet continue to run for a while. The number next to Running... should surpass 600. Is the simulation done? Is it stable or not? If it is changing, what can you say about the rate of change? Does the behavior of the simulation seem to fit reality?

8) While the applet is still running, click on the "Fixed" checkbox again to uncheck it. Click once on the red square in the legend. Then click on the red cell in the middle of your diagram. Since it is no longer fixed, its value can change. Remember that any cell that is fixed has a little white corner.

Describe what happens to your simulation now. Does this make sense to you? That is, does it accord with your intuition about the physical world?

Deliverables

Turn in four screenshots from the "Game of Life" applet. Also, turn in one screenshot from the "Heat transfer" applet, along with your answers to the preceding questions.

If you are running Heat or Life as standalone Java applications, save your files. Your instructor may want you to hand them in. Consult the instructor for details on how to do this.

Deeper Investigation

The "Heat transfer" applet is an archetype of many simulation programs, from weather to stellar clusters to fluid dynamics. Your textbook shows the variables and equations that govern meteorological models on p. 461. Pretty scary, huh? Write down what variables you might need to include in a stellar cluster model, and which ones you should include in a fluid dynamics model.

The Game of Life is identical to Heat in principle, but unlike Heat, it seems to give more bizarre, unpredictable results. Speculate on why this might be the case, based on what you know about the underlying game's rules and variables. (Hint: Think of what kinds of numbers are involved, namely reals or integers.)

Laboratory

Networking

15

Objectives

- Study how networks route packets to various destination hosts.
- Learn how networks ensure reliable delivery.

References

Software needed:

1) A web browser (Internet Explorer or Netscape)
2) Applets from the CD-ROM:
    a) TCP/IP
    b) Network router

Textbook reference: Chapter 15, pp. 476–483, 488–491

Background

Chapter 15, "Networks," explains the basic concepts; this lab elaborates on two aspects of computer networking.

Activity

Part 1

Though we tend to take networks for granted (except when they're down!), they are surprisingly complicated. Setting one up involves much more than just running a wire between two computers. Not only must the machines agree on a whole series of protocols and identifying conventions before any communication can happen, but the wire itself is subject to seemingly malevolent forces working to corrupt the fragile data traveling through it!

The TCP/IP protocol suite is a whole system of software, protocols, and management decisions. At its heart are several protocols that break messages into packets and send them from source computers to destination computers. In this activity, we will see a simplified form of TCP (Transmission Control Protocol) as it reliably sends a message to a destination computer.

Start the "TCP/IP" applet. This applet simulates a reliable connection, which means that a big message is correctly sent in its entirety from source to destination. If anything goes wrong, the software makes heroic attempts to recover the information. While it is impossible to absolutely guarantee that the message will arrive intact, the networking software can make it very likely that it will be delivered correctly.

In this applet, there are only two hosts, or nodes, numbered 0 and 1. Host 0 is a computer that is trying to send *your message* to host 1. You will play the role of one of those malevolent forces of nature, damaging and even destroying data packets. Will the software recover the data properly and save the day? Let's hope so!

Click on the *Example* button, which inserts a message into the *Your message* text area. Click *Run*, and then *Send a message*. Host 0 moves the message to the *To be sent* area and proceeds to "packetize" it into 10 character packets. Here you can see the first

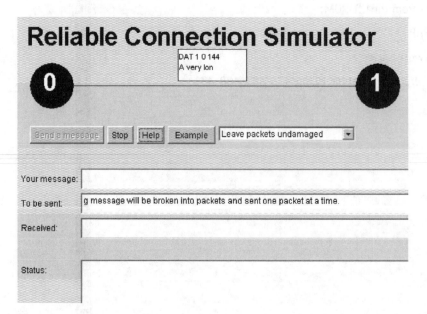

10 characters—`A very lon` (the two spaces are part of the count)—moving slowly in a packet across the wire.

What exactly does the `DAT 1 0 144` in the packet mean? This is the packet's *header* and contains crucial information. First, `DAT` identifies the type of packet being sent. There are three types of packets: `DAT` for *data*, `ACK` for *acknowledgment*, and `NAK` for *negative acknowledgment*. We will talk more about these in a minute.

Next in the header comes the *destination address*, which is 1. Though this seems a bit silly in a two-node network, bigger networks obviously require a destination address. The number 0, which appears next, is the *sequence number*. As messages are broken into packets, each packet is assigned a number: 0 in the first packet, 1 in the second packet, and so forth. If any packet were to arrive out of order, the destination computer could examine these sequence numbers and re-assemble the message in the correct order. After all, if part of the message were scrambled the meaning could change completely ("You owe us $1000" means something quite different from "You owe us 000$1".)

Finally, `144` is the *checksum*, which alerts the destination computer that the packet was damaged. This applet uses an extremely simple checksum algorithm, merely taking the ASCII value of each character in the packet, adding these together, and performing modulo 256 (keep the remainder after dividing by 256) so that the checksum is always between 0 and 255, inclusive. This checksum algorithm was actually used in some early protocols, but is prone to serious problems. Nowadays more advanced ones are used, most notably the *cyclic redundancy code*. We'd tell you how it works, but that would change our lab into an advanced mathematics class!

After the first packet arrives at host 1, it sends back an `ACK` packet to acknowledge that the data arrived successfully. The type of the packet is `ACK`; the destination is 0 (host 0), and the sequence number that it sends back is 1, meaning that it expects host 0 to send it a packet with the sequence number 1 next. Finally, there is no real data in an `ACK` packet, so the checksum is 0. This explains why the header is `ACK 0 1 0`.

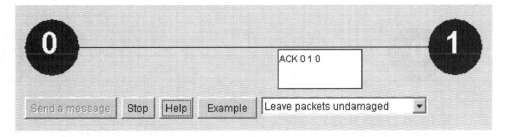

Networks are always contending with the forces of chaos that can corrupt the data being sent: noise on the line, equipment failures, and other sorts of mayhem. So let's wreak havoc on our poor little network and see what happens. Select *Damage packets that are touched* from the pull-down menu. You can do this while the applet is sending packets.

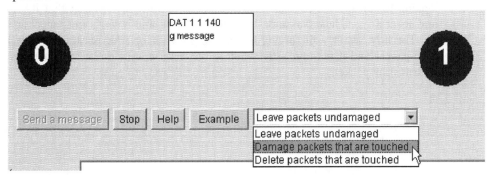

As a packet comes sliding along the wire, click on it with the mouse. This should somehow corrupt the data. For example, the s below turned into the Japanese yen symbol!

What does host 1 do when this packet arrives? How does it even know that the packet is damaged? It re-computes the checksum using the data it receives, and it matches the checksum in the header with the re-computed one. They don't match this time, so host 1 sends host 0 a NAK packet with the same sequence number. This tells host 0 that the packet was corrupted and needs to be re-sent.

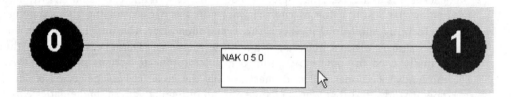

When Host 0 gets the NAK, it re-sends the packet. Various status messages appear in the large text area at the bottom of the applet, explaining what is going on.

Now let's experiment with more ways to make life difficult. Select *Delete packets that are touched* from the pull-down menu. When another packet comes along, click on it with your mouse and it should disappear.

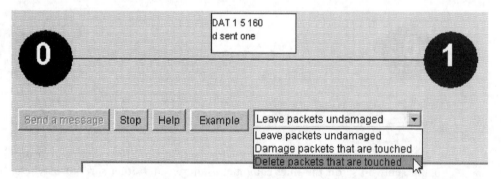

Packets that do not even arrive pose a bigger challenge than ones that are damaged. How does host 1 ever know that a packet is missing? Actually, it doesn't, but host 0 is looking for an ACK or NAK packet in response to each DAT packet that it sends. So if one never arrives, host 0 assumes the packet is lost, and it sends the packet again.

The host won't wait forever to receive the ACK or NAK packet It sets a timer on each packet and if nothing arrives before the timer counts down to 0, it *times out* and re-sends the packet.

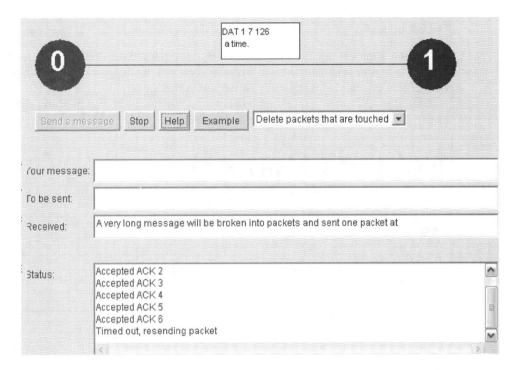

Of course, all of this assumes that everything, including the hosts and the software, is working correctly to catch any errors that may occur. As you can imagine, there are about a million things that can happen to foul up this pretty picture, and we will explore some of them in the exercise. But consider this: What if the packets are temporarily held up somehow? They aren't lost, but the timer goes off anyway. So what does host 1 do when it gets a duplicate packet? And does it send another ACK? Yikes! This networking is rapidly spinning out of control! Scientists who designed the Internet had to think about all these possibilities and decide how to handle them. Fortunately, they found reliable solutions so today we can sit in the comfort of our homes and travel the entire world with our fingertips.

Part 2

The second applet simulates how computers *route* packets to their final destinations. Routing is enormously complicated because there are so many variables. We will see some of this unexpected complexity as we watch this applet.

Start the "Network router" applet. Let's go for the most complex example right away. Select *Example 5* from the pull-down menu.

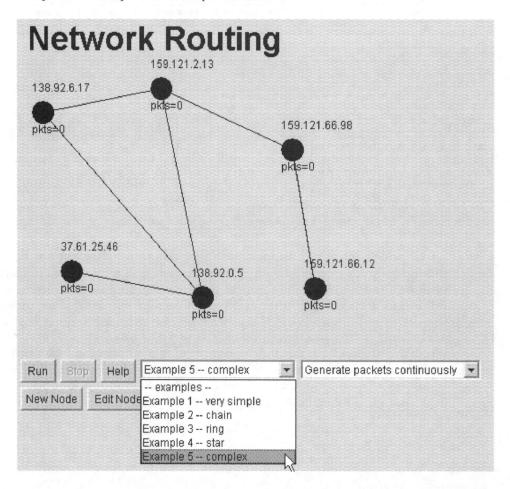

Each blue disk represents a node, or a computer in the network. The lines between nodes are telecommunication lines, perhaps telephone wires or Ethernet cables. Each node has its own IP address, a 32-bit number that is always represented as four octets separated by dots (see textbook pp. 488–489).

In this applet, the lines are *full duplex*, which means that packets can flow in either direction between the two connected hosts. This isn't always the case in the real world, but many lines are full duplex.

You can move the nodes around on the screen by dragging them. Their attached lines move with them. You can even add new nodes. To make a new node, double-click on any open space and the applet places there a blue dot with the unusable address of 0.0.0.0. You are expected to change that right away!

To change the characteristics of a node, double-click on the node and a new window appears:

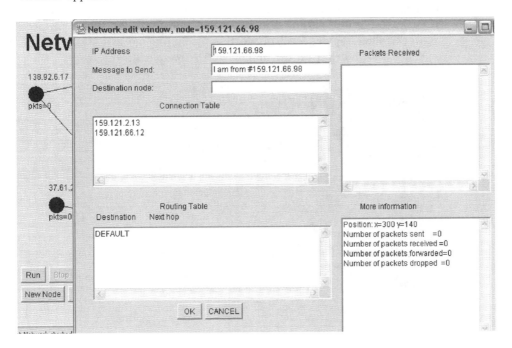

This window displays status information in the right column, showing packets that this node has received and some statistics. At the top are three fields that you can change, the first being the IP address of the node. You can also customize the message you want to send, and you can add the address of the recipient. If the *Destination node* field is blank, no messages will be sent by this node. More than one node can send and receive messages at the same time when this applet runs.

The connection and routing tables below these fields are the focus of this applet's study. The connection table lists the IP addresses of nodes that *directly connect* to this node. Most networks assume, quite logically, that two nodes can find each other and send packets if they are directly connected. It is when nodes are not directly connected to their destinations that things get interesting!

The purpose of the routing table is to tell the node what to do when it is not directly connected to the destination node. For example, if node X wants to send a packet to node Y, which is not directly connected, it must send the packet to node Z instead, and node Z then assumes the responsibility of getting it to node Y. Hopefully, Z will not mistakenly send it back to X! If so, a *routing loop* would occur and the packet would travel the wires endlessly, like the Flying Dutchman. This prospect so worried early developers of TCP/IP that they put a timer on each packet so that it would just evaporate after going through too many nodes.

The routing table has two columns. The first column lists the destination, and the second lists the next hop. The next hop must be a directly connected node. There are also a number of special cases that can shorten routing tables. If the word DEFAULT appears in the routing table, then the node merely sends packets to the first node in the directly connected table. This works nicely for *leaf* nodes, which connect to only one other node, but won't work for a complex topology (*topology* refers to the configuration of the network; various topologies are shown on p. 478 of your text).

Most of the time, nodes with two or more connections need to explicitly list all distant nodes, along with the next hop. However, this quickly gets tedious and requires too much work to update, as many new nodes are added. One possible alternative is to list some of the destination/next hop pairs, and leave the others unspecified. The "Network router" applet lets you do this by putting an asterisk in the destination column, as shown below for the ring network (*Example 3*):

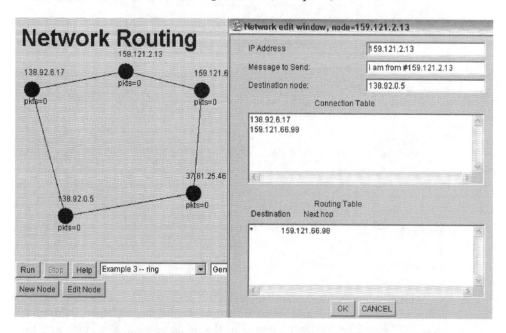

Finally, what can we do if the network is under attack and the routing table is now obsolete due to out-of-commission routers? Early TCP/IP developers worried about this, too, and came up with the *hot potato algorithm*. This applet allows you to type HOT POTATO in the routing table. Nothing else is needed. Hot potato works this way: When a packet comes in, the node makes a random guess as to which directly connected node will get the packet to its final destination, and it sends it to that next hop. This may not work and it may result in routing loops, but it just might do the trick, too. Imagine a bunch of people on the beach around a campfire passing around a hot sweet potato wrapped in aluminum foil. As they energetically toss it to one another, there is a good chance that it will end up in the hands (or lap) of someone who wants to eat it!

There are many other routing algorithms that were designed with various emergencies or unusual conditions in mind. One such algorithm is called *flooding*, in which every packet is copied to every outgoing wire, not just to one random one, as in hot potato.

What happens in the Internet, which is built on TCP/IP? What routing algorithms are used? The local area networks that attach to the Internet often use specialized routing algorithms. For example, Ethernet is like a party-line telephone where everyone can hear everyone else's calls. So when the phone rings, or a new packet comes in, each computer listens to the beginning of the packet to see if it is meant for them.

The backbone network that manages the long-distance, high-volume traffic on the Internet uses several *dynamic* routing protocols. In such systems, nodes change their routing tables from time to time as they are forwarding packets. Unlike the "Network router" applet, in which you, the *network administrator*, decide once and for all what the routing table for node X is, dynamic routing systems measure the characteristics of the traffic and the attached lines, and adjust their routing tables so that packets will flow most efficiently through the entire system. This sounds daunting and it is, kind of like continuously adjusting the timing on all traffic lights so that cars on the streets get to their destinations in the least amount of time. While the system isn't perfect, it's worked on the Internet for over 30 years.

Exercise 1

Name _____ Date _____

Section _____

1) Start the "TCP/IP" (reliable connection simulator) applet.

2) In the textfield labeled "Your message:", type the following:

   Computer networking is essential in our world today.

   Then press the button "Send a message."

3) Watch the entire sequence of packets that are sent for the sample message. How many DAT packets were sent? How many ACK packets were sent?

4) If each character or blank in a packet header counts for one character, and all DAT packets except the last carry 10 characters, and ACK packets have no data characters (though they do have a header), count up how many characters were sent in total.

5) There are 52 characters in the *Example* message, including blanks and punctuation. Subtract 52 from the total number of characters sent in both directions in all packets. (Do not damage or delete packets this time.) Divide this number by the total number of characters to get the *overhead*, expressed as a percentage.

6) Imagine that you have a million-character message to send, perhaps a large file. How many characters total would be sent in all packets necessary to move it from node 0 to node 1?

7) What would be an obvious way to decrease the overhead? Why might this solution backfire? Under what conditions?

Exercise 2

Name _____ Date _____

Section _____

1) Repeat Steps 1 and 2 from Exercise 1.

2) Select *Delete packets that are touched.*

3) Delete some data packets by clicking on them as they move along the wire and watch the re-transmission after timeout.

4) What happens if you delete the re-transmitted packet? Does the "TCP/IP" applet need to take any special action?

5) Now try deleting some ACK or NAK packets. What happens?

Exercise 3

Name _____ Date _____

Section _____

1) See if you can compute the checksum as TCP/IP does. Run the applet, using any message. Select a data packet, but don't select the last packet because it might be too short—less than 10 characters.

2) Count up the characters, including blanks. If they do not equal 10, assume there are blanks at the end so that the character count is 10.

3) Using the "Text Translator into ASCII" applet from Lab 3b, type in the characters from the data packet, and click on *translate text*. (You can use an ASCII chart instead if you'd prefer.)

4) Add up the values for each of the characters. Then take the modulus of this number using 256. The modulus operator is available on some computer calculators and is represented by *mod*, but you can easily compute it by dividing the total by 256 and saving only the remainder. For instance, suppose the total is 7452. Since $7452 \div 256 = 29.109375$, but we only want the remainder. Multiply 0.109375 by 256, which gives us 28. Or: $7452 - (29 \times 256) = 28$.

5) Compare your computed checksum against what the applet shows for the packet. Do they agree?

6) Now damage your packet by altering one character. Re-compute the checksum. Do you see how TCP/IP can spot errors?

7) Think of a way that a packet can be damaged and still have the same checksum as the undamaged version. (There are several possibilities. Imagine that two or more bytes are altered at the same time.)

Exercise 4

Name _____   Date _____

Section _____

1) Start the "Network router" applet. Select *Example 3*, the ring network.

2) Become familiar with the applet. Move a few nodes around by dragging them.

3) Double-click on the node 37.61.25.46. List the nodes it is directly connected to.

4) If 37.61.25.46 wants to send packets to a node that is not directly connected, to which node will it first send the packets? (Check the routing table by double clicking on the node.)

5) Run the applet for a while, letting it generate packets continuously. Double-click on 37.61.25.46 again and look at its statistics. How many packets were sent? Received? Forwarded?

6) Who else is sending messages, and to whom?

7) Click on 138.92.6.17. Write down its statistics.

Exercise 5

Name _____ Date _____

Section _____

1) Start the "Network router" applet. Select *Example 4*, the star network.

2) Look at the routing and connection tables for the center node and several other nodes. Describe any pattern you can see in these tables.

3) How is the connection table for the center node different from the other nodes?

4) Select *Generate when I click on a node* from the pull-down menu. This means a user at this computer wants to send packets to the 126.14.5.46 computer.

5) If you double-click on 159.121.2.13, you will see that its destination node is 126.14.5.46. Run the applet, click on 159.121.2.13, and watch the packets go. What color does the sending computer turn briefly? What color does the destination computer turn? What does it mean if a node flashes green?

6) Many early computer networks used the star topology (*Example 4* on the applet). What will happen if the center node in this type of network dies?

Exercise 6

Name _____ Date _____

Section _____

1) Start the "Network router" applet but don't select an example network.

2) Click on the "New Node" button four times, which will place four nodes on your screen. Move them around into a square. Then double click on node 0.0.0.1. When the edit window appears, type the IP addresses of the other nodes into the Connection Table, as shown:

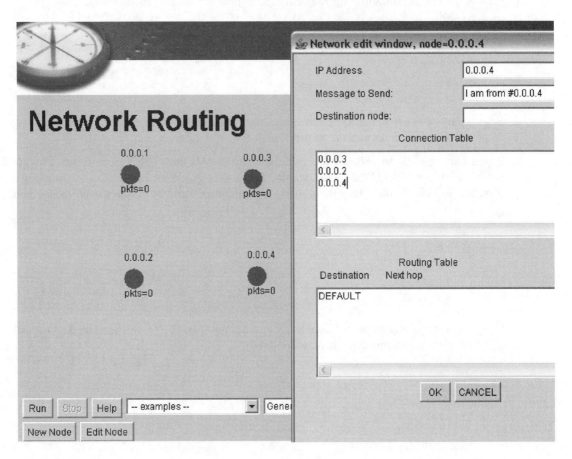

3) Now edit nodes 0.0.0.2, 0.0.0.3, and 0.0.0.4. In each case, add every other node to their Connection Tables. When you are done, every node will have a direct wire to every other node:

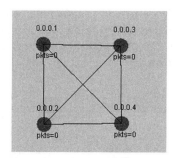

This is what is called a *directly connected network*. It is also called a *fully connected network*, for obvious reasons. Every node in the network has a direct connection to every other node. Is there a need for a routing table in this network?

4) Sketch out below a network of 2 nodes and make it directly connected. Do not bother to assign address numbers to the nodes. Just draw circles with lines between them.

5) Now sketch out a network of 3 nodes and directly connect every node.

6) Fill in the table below, which compares the number of nodes in a directly connected network to the total number of wires in the network. Do not double count wires between the same nodes. That is, since there is a wire between 0.0.0.1 and 0.0.0.2, there is also a wire going the other direction, from 0.0.0.2 to 0.0.0.1. Count this as just one wire, not 2.

Number of nodes	Total number of wires
2	_____
3	_____
4	_____

7) Make a prediction for a 5-node network.

8) Now click on New Node to add a new node, whose number will be 0.0.0.5. Edit the other four nodes and add 0.0.0.5 to their Connection Tables. Once you are done, move your nodes around so that the nodes sit at the corners of a pentagon, as shown below. (Not all wires are shown.)

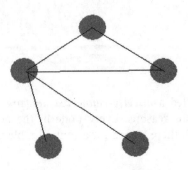

9) Fill in the table for 5. Did your guess match the final network?

10) Either sketch a 6-node network by hand or use the applet, building on your 5-node network. Complete the previous table by filling in the total number of wires. Are you surprised?

11) List one major advantage of a directly connected network.

12) List one major disadvantage of a directly connected network.

13) The telephone system is a network where each telephone is a node in the network. Do you imagine that the telephone system is a directly connected network? If not, why not?

Deliverables

· ·

Turn in your hand-written answers.

Deeper Investigation

· ·

One possible network topology is the *fully connected network*. In this topology, every node has a direct line to every other node. This would be ideal for speed! Draw five nodes and fully connect the network. What is the downside of this topology?

Draw fully connected networks for sizes two, three, four, six, and 10 nodes. Can you figure out a formula that predicts how many lines will be needed if there are *n* nodes in the network?

Fully connected networks are too costly in general (imagine every computer in the whole world having a direct wire to every other computer!). But star networks and others are not *fault tolerant*; they isolate some computers if one or more nodes dies or a communication wire breaks. Can you invent a network topology that is not fully connected, yet provides redundancy so that every node has at least two paths to other nodes?

First Steps in HTML

Objective

- Learn some basic HTML concepts.
- Make a simple web page.

References

Software needed:

1) A basic text editor (for example, NotePad on a PC or SimpleText on a Mac) to create the web page

2) A web browser (Internet Explorer or Netscape Navigator, for example) to view the HTML page

You'll also need a disk or some other means of saving your work. Check with your lab instructor for details.

Please note: For this lab, avoid using software that automatically generates the HTML tags (such as Microsoft Word, PageMill, Dreamweaver, etc.)—you want to get a taste of working "under the hood" with the actual HTML code.

Textbook reference: pp. 507–512

Background

Chapter 16, "The World Wide Web," discusses the basics of HTML, and the Activity section below introduces the skills necessary for this lab.

Activity

For this lab you'll create a simple web page using HTML (HyperText Markup Language). HTML is the basic language of web pages. The designer of a web page uses HTML "tags" to describe the general structure of the page. These tags identify various elements of the page (titles, headings, paragraphs, etc.), along with character formatting information (bold, italic, etc.). Once the elements of the page are defined using the tags, a web browser interprets these tags to determine how to display the web page on a computer screen.

For example, let's say the browser sees this collection of text and tags in HTML:

```
<H1>Welcome to My Page!</H1>
```

Notice the first tag: <H1>. All tags are surrounded by angle brackets in this fashion. This first tag is HTML code for a heading (like a headline). There are six different levels of headings in HTML, H1 through H6. H1 is the largest and most prominent heading.

The <H1> tag "turns on" the heading formatting. All the text following this tag will be in the boldest heading format, until another tag "turns off" the formatting. Immediately following the first tag is the phrase Welcome to My Page! A browser would show that text in a bold and prominent way, due to the <H1> tag.

The text is followed by another tag: </H1>. Notice the slash before the H1. The slash is used to designate "stop" tags: This is the tag that "turns off" the heading formatting, so that subsequent text will not be formatted as a heading. Most tags function like this, with a "start" tag that designates the beginning of a section, feature, or formatting, and a "stop" tag with a slash in it that designates the end of the section, feature, or formatting.

Here, then, is how <H1>Welcome to My Page!</H1> might actually be interpreted by a browser:

Welcome to My Page!

As the biggest and boldest heading in HTML, it pretty much "screams" on the page!

To further understand how HTML works, we'll make a practice page. Start by launching your text editor, which should bring up a blank page on your screen. Carefully type the following code:

```
<HTML>
<HEAD>
<TITLE>Practice Page</TITLE>
</HEAD>
<BODY>
```

These first tags are the basic structural tags that should begin every HTML page. The <HTML> tag announces to the browser that the document is in HTML code. The <HEAD> tag is a structural tag for the header of the document. The most common element of the header is the <TITLE> of the document. Notice the text surrounded by the <TITLE> and </TITLE> tags—this text would appear in the title bar at the top of the browser window. Notice how the ⟨TITLE⟩ start and stop tags are nested within the ⟨HEAD⟩ start and stop tags.

The main contents of the page appear after the ⟨BODY⟩ tag. Everything following this tag would appear in the main portion of the browser window.

Your HTML document should end with the following two stop tags–type them in now:

```
</BODY>
</HTML>
```

Let's return to the discussion of headings in HTML. To see how your browser handles the various heading tags, open up some space between the ⟨BODY⟩ and ⟨/BODY⟩ tags in your document, and type the following code:

```
<H1>This is Heading 1</H1>
<H2>This is Heading 2</H2>
<H3>This is Heading 3</H3>
<H4>This is Heading 4</H4>
<H5>This is Heading 5</H5>
<H6>This is Heading 6</H6>
```

We are using our text editor to create our code, of course, but now we want to view our work with a browser, like Microsoft Internet Explorer or Netscape Navigator, to see what our HTML code looks like when a browser renders it as a web page. Before you can view your code in a browser, though, you need to save it to disk. We'll do that now: Go to your text editor's *File* menu and choose *Save*. Call this file practice.htm. (If you're not sure what disk or where on the disk you are to save your file, consult your lab instructor.)

Once you've saved your file with your text editor, launch your browser, go to the *File* menu, and choose *Open*. Find your way to the saved practice.htm file and open it. You should see the six sizes of headings. It will look something like the screenshot below (note the name **Practice Page** in the title bar of the browser window—this was the text that was between the start and stop ⟨TITLE⟩ tags):

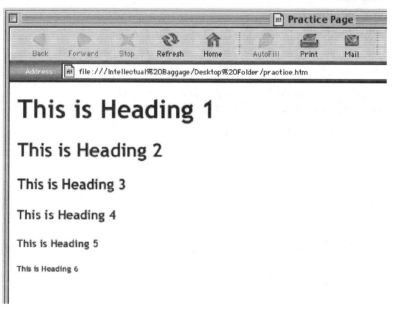

(By the way, the exact appearance of an HTML page can vary from browser to browser. While this lack of uniformity drives serious web designers nuts, it ensures that almost any computer, regardless of what fonts are installed on it, will be able to format and display HTML pages.)

Throughout the rest of this lab, you'll go back and forth between the text editor, where you'll edit your HTML page, and the browser, where you'll view your changes. (**Important note:** Make sure to never try to save your page while viewing it in the browser—your browser may save the page in a format that your text editor can't open!)

You designate paragraphs in an HTML document with the paragraph tag: ⟨P⟩. This tag informs the browser to leave some space in front of whatever block of text it precedes. Return to your page in the text editor and type the following code after the headers and before the ⟨/BODY⟩ tag:

```
<P>This is my first paragraph.</P>

<P>This is my second paragraph.</P>
```

(It's worth noting that tags are *not* case-sensitive—you can make them lowercase if you'd like. We're going to keep ours uppercase to make them stand out more in our code, so it is easier to read. However, the new XHTML standard, which will eventually replace HTML, explicitly says they must be lowercase. Like many things in Computer Science, learn today, revise tomorrow.)

Now you'll view your changes. Save your work in the text editor, return to the browser, and click the *Reload* or *Refresh* button (or reopen the file from the browser's *File* menu if you closed it). You should see your new paragraphs in the browser window.

Return to your page in the text editor. Now let's take a quick look at lists in HTML. The two most commonly used lists in HTML are *ordered* and *unordered*. Here's a screenshot of a heading followed by an unordered list:

My Favorite Jazz Musicians

- Charles Mingus
- Miles Davis
- Sonny Rollins
- John Coltrane
- Thelonious Monk

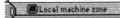 Local machine zone

Here's the HTML code for the above list:

```
<H3>My Favorite Jazz Musicians</H3>

<UL>

<LI>Charles Mingus

<LI>Miles Davis

<LI>Sonny Rollins

<LI>John Coltrane

<LI>Thelonious Monk

</UL>
```

Notice from the screenshot that in an unordered list the browser puts a bullet (•) in front of each item in the list.

Take a look at how the code for this list works. The ⟨UL⟩ tag announces to the browser that an unordered list (*unordered* meaning *not numbered*) is about to begin. The ⟨LI⟩ tag is used to announce each individual list item. (Important note: ⟨LI⟩ stands for "List Item"–notice that it's the letter *L* and the letter *I*, not the letter *L* and the number *1*!) After all the items in the list have been entered, the unordered list feature is turned off using the ⟨/UL⟩ tag. (Notice that the ⟨LI⟩ tag does not have a corresponding "stop" tag; it's one of only a few HTML tags that doesn't take a stop tag–this will also change in the new XHTML standard, which requires the stop tag.)

What if you wanted the list to be numbered? You'd simply tell the browser to create an ordered list instead of an unordered list, by replacing the ⟨UL⟩ and ⟨/UL⟩ tags with the ⟨OL⟩ and ⟨/OL⟩ tags. Note that the ⟨LI⟩ tags remain unchanged. Making that simple change to the preceding code would make the list look like this:

My Favorite Jazz Musicians

1. Charles Mingus
2. Miles Davis
3. Sonny Rollins
4. John Coltrane
5. Thelonious Monk

Local machine zone

Again, note that the ⟨LI⟩ tags are not changed at all–the browser inserts the numbers 1 through 5 that appear in the list above. These numbers are not actually written in the HTML code.

Add a simple unordered list (list anything you'd like) on your practice page, then save it and view it in your browser. Then go back to your page in the text editor and change the ⟨UL⟩ and ⟨/UL⟩ tags to ⟨OL⟩ and ⟨/OL⟩. Save your work, view your page in your browser again, and note the difference.

Finally, we'll mention some simple text formatting tags, for bold and italic text. Like the heading tags, the text formatting tags must be turned on and then turned off with the appropriate start and stop tags. To create bold or italic text, surround the text to be affected with the appropriate tags. In the case of bold text, here's a sample line of code:

```
<B>This text will appear bold.</B>.
```

Here's how your browser interprets that line of code:

This text will appear bold.

To make italicized text, use the start and stop ⟨I⟩ tags instead:

```
<I>This text will appear in italics.</I>.
```

Here's how it will look:

This text will appear in italics.

Experiment with these tags on your practice page.

Exercise 1

Name _____   Date _____

Section _____

While you're obviously not ready to become a freelance web designer, you *are* ready to make a simple web page. For this lab, you'll be creating a simple biography web page.

Your page should include a brief biographical sketch of yourself. Include the following information:

- Where you're from
- What your major is
- What your plans are after graduation
- What you hope to be doing 10 years from now

Also include a brief discussion of your hobbies and interests outside of school. Be creative: If you're an avid hiker or biker, a vegetarian, a world traveler, an expert knitter, a bassoonist, an excellent cook, or a national champion hog caller, tell your story (or stories...). And hey, if there are any oddities about yourself ("My eyes are two different colors" or "You should see my barbed wire collection" or "I was raised by the Borg"), mention them on your page!

You should also create a couple of lists on your page; some possible topics include:

- Your favorite musical groups
- Your favorite foods
- Your most despised foods
- Your favorite books
- Your favorite TV shows

Almost anything that can be put into a list format can be included here.

Deliverables

When you're satisfied with your page, view it with the browser and print it from the browser's *File* menu. Hand in the printout of your page as it appears in the browser. Your lab instructor might also want you to hand in an electronic copy of your file—check with your instructor for details.

Laboratory 16B

Linking & Images in HTML

Objectives

....

■ Expand on the basic HTML skills you learned in Lab 16A.

■ Work with links and images in HTML.

References

....

Lab 16A must be completed before working on this lab—you'll be modifying the HTML biography page created in that lab.

Software needed:

1) A basic text editor (for example, NotePad on a PC or SimpleText on a Mac) to create the web page

2) A web browser (Internet Explorer or Netscape Navigator, for example) to view the HTML page

You'll also need a disk or some other means of saving your work. Check with your lab instructor for details.

Textbook reference: pp. 507–512

Background

You already learned the basic structural, heading, list-making, and text formatting tags in HTML in Lab 16A. The Activity section below explains what you need to know for this lab.

Activity

Now that you've created a basic web page, you'll be learning a few more HTML skills:

- How to link to another page you've created.
- How to link to other sites on the Web.
- How to incorporate images into your web page.

First, let's talk about how HTML pages differ from other media, such as a novel. A best-seller provides a tried-and-true method for presenting information. A reader experiences the words in a *linear* fashion, starting on page 1 and progressing page by page through to the end of the book. If you've ever been moved by a skilled author, you know this can be a highly effective way to express ideas.

HTML permits the organization of information using a different paradigm. The presentation of information in HTML can be especially interesting and compelling because it can be experienced in a *non-linear*, user-directed fashion. While reading a web page, a reader encounters links embedded in the document, triggered by key words or phrases called *hyperlinks*. These links will take the reader to new web pages that somehow expand on or are related to the concepts implied by the key words—if the reader chooses to follow them! With HTML, readers access information as they wish, depending on their interests, following some links and ignoring others.

Words that function as links in HTML stand out from the rest of the text. The default way that most browsers display links is as underlined, blue text. While web designers can tweak the appearance of links (to appear in other colors, for instance), most at least reserve underlined text for links because users have come to expect underlined text to function in this way.

Linking in HTML is done with the ⟨A⟩ (called "anchor") tag. This tag both changes the appearance of the text it surrounds and turns that text into a link. Here's the typical code for a link:

```
<A HREF="page2.html">Go to Page 2</A>
```

Let's look it over and see what it does. The A specifies the anchor tag, used for links. HREF (short for "hypertext reference") is an *attribute* of the anchor tag, meaning it modifies the tag. This is followed by an equals sign and a value in quotes, ="page2.html", which specifies where the link should take the user. That's the end of the start ⟨A⟩ tag. This tag has "turned on" the linking feature, and any text that follows it will be affected until the stop tag turns off the feature. So the text after the start tag, Go to Page 2, will appear in the browser as a link—usually underlined and blue, as we've mentioned.

Finally, the stop tag, ⟨/A⟩, turns off the linking feature. Notice that the stop anchor tag does not include the attribute inside it—no HREF or address is listed in it. Stop tags don't take attributes.

The address in quotes in the above code is called a *relative* address—it resides in the same folder as the page linking to it. As you know, web pages can also link to different sites entirely, using *absolute* addresses. Contrast the relative address in the tag above with the absolute address used below:

```
<A HREF="http://www.cnn.com">Visit the CNN web site.</A>
```

Notice that the absolute address on the preceding page is the complete URL of the referenced page. When referencing an "outside" page, it's necessary to provide a complete address so the browser knows where to find it.

To show you the use of anchor tags "in action," here's a screenshot of a page with links, followed by the actual source code for the page:

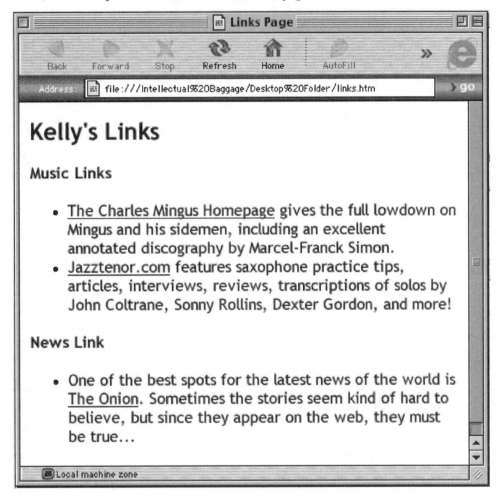

```
<HTML>
<HEAD>
<TITLE>Links Page</TITLE>
</HEAD>
<BODY>
<H2>Kelly's Links</H2>
<H4>Music Links</H4>
<UL>
<LI>
<A HREF="http://www.siba.fi/~eonttone/mingus">
```

The Charles Mingus Homepage</A> gives the full lowdown on Mingus and his sidemen, including an excellent annotated discography by Marcel-Franck Simon.

```
<LI><A HREF="http://www.jazztenor.com">
```

Jazztenor.com</A> features saxophone practice tips, articles, interviews, reviews, transcriptions of solos by John Coltrane, Sonny Rollins, Dexter Gordon, and more!

```
</UL>
<H4>News Link</H4>
<UL>
<LI>One of the best spots for the latest news of the world is
<A HREF="http://www.theonion.com">The Onion</A>. Sometimes the
stories seem kind of hard to believe, but since they appear on
the web, they must be true...
</UL>
</BODY>
</HTML>
```

Study the above code to make sure you understand how anchor tags are used in web pages.

In addition to working with links, for this lab you'll also be adding an image to a web page. To make an image appear on a web page, HTML code that tells the browser where the image can be found is added to the page. The browser then hunts down the image and displays it in the appropriate spot on the page. (The image must be in a format supported by the browser. The two most widely supported formats are JPEG and GIF. These formats are briefly discussed on p. 79 of your textbook.)

This differs from the way an image is incorporated into a word-processing document (a Microsoft Word file, for example). In a Word file, the image is actually embedded into the file itself. By contrast, in an HTML document, the browser is referred to the image's URL on the server; the browser loads this image from the server and displays it on the screen in the appropriate place in the HTML file.

The <IMG> tag, called the image tag, is used in the code for images. Here's an example:

```
<IMG SRC="myphoto.jpg">
```

IMG of course specifies the image tag, and SRC is the attribute that signals to the browser that what follows is the address of the image. After the equals sign, the value "myphoto.jpg" which is the name of the image. appears in quotation marks.

Just as with links, image tags can use relative or absolute addresses. Because the address in our image tag above includes only the name of the file, with no additional navigational information, our browser will assume that the file is in the same directory as the HTML page referring to it.

Here's an example of an image tag referring to an outside, absolute address:

```
<IMG SRC="http://www.mysite.com/photos/myphoto.jpg">
```

Please note that there is no stop tag for the <IMG> tag.

Exercise 1

Name _____ Date _____

Section _____

You will be modifying a copy of your biography web page from Lab 16A. Before you begin, you need to:

1) Make a new directory (folder) on your disk, called `YourLastNameLab16b`. (Of course, substitute *your* last name for `YourLastName`! For example, Meyer Lab16b.)

2) Make a copy of your web page from Lab 16A. The copy of the file should be called `index.htm`.

3) Put `index.htm` into your new directory.

   Note: From this point on, we will refer to the `index.htm` page as your **home page**.

4) You'll also need to put a JPEG image into your Lab 16b directory. If you have your own JPEG image, you can use that; otherwise, a sample JPEG image (called `lab16b.jpg`) is available on the CD-Rom. Your lab instructor can show you how to copy this practice image into your Lab 16b directory.

Exercise 2

Name _____ Date _____

Section _____

1) Open your home page with your text editor.

2) Open a new line immediately after the ⟨BODY⟩ tag near the top of your HTML document, and add a line of code that will make the JPEG image appear on your web page. (If you're using the image provided on the CD-ROM, it's called lab16b.jpg; if you're using your own image, you'll need to use the name of your image as part of the tag.)

3) Save your home page in your text editor. (It should still be called index.htm.)

4) View your home page in your browser (as described in Lab 16A).

(Please note: As long as your JPEG image and your home page are in the same folder, you should see the image appear at the top of your page when viewing it with your browser.)

Exercise 3

Name _____   Date _____

Section _____

1) From within your text editor, go to the *File* menu and choose *New*. A blank text document will appear.

2) Go to the *File* menu and choose *Save As*.

3) In the *Save* dialog box that appears on your screen, route this document so that it is saved in your Lab 16B directory.

4) Name this new document `links.htm` (make sure there are no spaces in the name, and use lowercase letters).

5) Click the *Save* button. From now on, we'll call this new page your **links page**.

6) Add the appropriate structural tags to set up your new links page, starting with ⟨HTML⟩. (Refer to your home page, or to the Activity section of Lab 16A, if you need a reminder of what the structural tags look like.)

7) Once you've got the appropriate structural tags in place, add a heading that says: YourName's Favorite Links. (Replace YourName with *your* name.)

8) Using the screenshot and code demonstrating the use of the ⟨A⟩ tag as a model, create your own simple links page showing a few sites you enjoy.

9) Test your new links page in the browser to make sure that it works. If you try clicking on a link in the browser and get an error message, check to make sure you have no typos in your code. (By the way, sometimes you'll get an error message when trying to visit another site because the server for that site is down. It doesn't happen often, but it is a possibility. If you're sure that there are no errors in your code and that you're online, and you're still getting an error message when you click on a link, it's possible that's the source of the problem.)

Exercise 4

Name _____ Date _____

Section _____

1) Open your home page with the text editor.

2) On your home page, add a new paragraph that says "Check out some of my favorite links" on a line just above the `</BODY>` tag toward the bottom of your document. Make the last three words of that sentence ("my favorite links") into a link that, when clicked on, will take you to your links page.

3) Save your work, and view it in your browser.

Exercise 5

Name _____ Date _____

Section _____

1) Add a link to your links page that, when clicked on, will take you to your home page.

Deliverables

Open your two web pages with your text editor and print them out, and then view them with your browser and print them again, for a total of four printouts. Your lab instructor might also want you to hand in an electronic copy of your file—check with your instructor for details.

Laboratory

Limits of Computing

17

Objectives

- Investigate the growth of mathematical functions.
- Watch the Traveling Salesperson find the best route.

References

Software needed:

1) A web browser (Internet Explorer or Netscape)

2) Applets from the CD-ROM:

    a) Comparison of several functions

    b) Plotter

    c) Traveling Salesperson Problem

Textbook reference: Chapter 17, pp. 528–534, 557–558

Background

Everything you need to learn is explained in Chapter 17, "Limitations of Computing."

Activity

Part 1

Chapter 17 discusses a fascinating variety of limitations on the power of computers. Many people seem to believe that computers are all-powerful, but this chapter will give you the intellectual tools to discard that notion. (Of course, we would not deny for a moment that computer *scientists* are all-knowing and all-powerful!)

For our first investigation, we'll use the "Comparison of several functions" applet to watch how large the values of functions can get. Start that applet and type 10 into the top field, next to N. The applet will calculate several functions of N and display their values. (See the screenshot below.)

Review the values in the white text areas and try to make sense of them. N*100 should be easy; just multiply the value in the N box by 100. The *caret symbol*, as in N^2, is used in some computer programs to signify exponentiation. Thus, N^2 means "raise N to the power of 2" or "multiply N by itself." We would normally see this in math textbooks as N^2. 2^N is quite a different matter! You can see that 2^N is usually much larger than N^2, so the exponentiation operator is by no means commutative. In this case, 2^N means "raise 2 to the power of N."

The logarithm function, notated log N, unnecessarily scares some people. All it really does is count the number of 0s after the 1, if the number is base 10. Thus, log 100,000 is 5. Another way of thinking about logarithms is to imagine they are exponents standing on their head. 10^5 is 100,000. Not so scary, huh?

Comparison of Several Functions

N	10
log N (truncated)	1
N * 100	1000
N * log(N) (truncated)	30
N^2	100
2^N	1024
N!	3628800
N^N	10000000000

f(N):		=	
f(N):		=	
f(N):		=	

Compute	Example 1	Example 2	Example 3	What is a function?

Part 2

Functions are interesting creatures. Some are tame and predictable while others are wild and exotic. Mathematicians capture and study them as if they were rare reptiles. Computer scientists, on the other hand, are interested in functions because they summarize the behavior of algorithms.

Every algorithm uses both time and space. It takes a certain number of instructions to find a solution to a problem, and the program needs a certain number of memory cells to find that solution. Functions describe these numbers in terms of how big the problem is.

In Part 1, we looked at functions numerically, which gave us insight as to how fast they grow. In this part, we use an applet that lets us draw plots of functions on an X-Y coordinate graph. The resulting lines and curves are visualizations of function behavior.

Start the "Plotter" applet and notice that there are the usual X and Y axes. The second pull-down menu lets you choose a function that has already been programmed in. Below shows the function log2(x), which is the logarithm base 2 of x, where x is a value on the X axis.

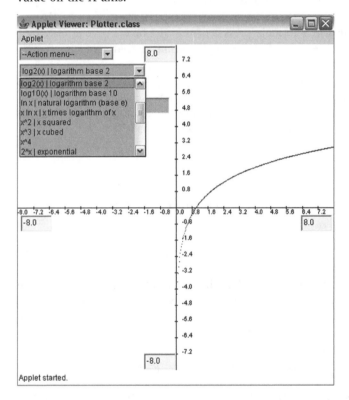

You can plot more than one function at a time. Doing so allows you to compare functions. For example, plot these functions together:

2x

x^2

2^x

The notation x^2 means "x raised to the second power" which is x times itself. You are more likely to see x^2 in a mathematics textbook. The caret symbol is sometimes used in place of superscripts, which are tricky to type on traditional keyboards.

The "Action" menu has a number of helpful options, including Help and Clear. Clear removes all currently plotted functions. You can also hide the axes, the yellow bounds boxes, and even the other boxes.

The yellow bounds boxes at the edges of the X and Y axes allow you to type in a new value. The top box holds the maximum Y, while the bottom box holds minimum Y. The left one holds minimum X and the right one maximum X. You can zero in on a particular part of the plot by appropriately setting those values.

Sometimes functions change so quickly that the line or curve is shown as a sequence of dots. These are the individual plot points representing the y value that the applet calculated for the X value underneath. To make the lines or curves smoother, increase the number of plot points in the box. Don't be afraid to make it exorbitantly large, like 30,000. Computers are so splendidly fast that you won't see a slowdown.

While the functions that this applet includes are interesting, it would be nice to enter your own, which you can do in the textfield labeled "Your formula:" There are two kinds of formulas you can type:

polynomials $\qquad 5x^3 - 3.2x^2 + x - 2.1$

Fourier series $\qquad 3\cos x - \sin 0.5x + 4.7\cos 13x$

After you have typed in a formula press *return* in the box. You can only plot one user formula at a time. There are four example formulas that you can select from the Choose Function pull-down.

Polynomials are powers of x, multiplied by real numbers. The powers can be integers, fractions, or negatives. However, if they are negatives, they must be enclosed in parentheses. Since you can't type superscripts in a textfield, use the caret symbol. Here are some valid polynomials that this applet accepts:

5x^3-3.2x^2+x-2.1

x^0.5 $\qquad\qquad$ (the same as the square root of x)

x^(-4) $\qquad\qquad$ (negative powers require parentheses)

Fourier series are sums of sines and cosines, which are periodic trigonometric functions. If all this terminology scares you, then just enjoy the beautiful pictures that mathematics paints.

First, clear all functions. Then select sin x from the pull-down function menu. No, that is not an exhortation to do something bad! Shame on you for thinking it! In fact, it is pronounced "sign-X" just like street sign. In full, it is spelled sine. cos is short for cosine, which is what you do to help a friend get a loan…no, wrong verb! Sorry. tan is short for tangent, which is what this book often goes off on!

All three of these trigonometric functions are *periodic*, which means they repeat themselves over and over forever. Sine and cosine are nice undulating waves, like the tide on the beach. In fact, sine and cosine have exactly the same shape. The only difference is that they are displaced differently on the X axis. If you could slide cosine so that it overlaps sine, you would see only one wave.

Tangent is a strange duck because, though it is periodic like its two prettier cousins, there are sharp breaks. It is not *continuous*. There is not one unbroken curve. Instead, every so often the tangent line veers off toward infinity or negative infinity and there isn't anything you can do about it.

Jean Baptiste Joseph Fourier, who was a child during the American Revolution, discovered that every periodic function, even those with warty or boxy shapes, could be broken down into a sum of sine and cosine functions. With the appropriate values, and enough sines and cosines, any period function can be displayed.

The applet's Example 4 is a sum of two cosine functions that gives a mildly interesting curve. To see it better, type 32 in the maximum X box and −32 in the minimum X box. Also change the number of plot points to 3000. Can you see the periodicity of the function?

Here are some Fourier series that this applet accepts:

sin x

cos x

5sin x + 2.6cos x

sin 0.5x − 3.8 sin 17.4x

In summary, this plotter applet allows you to visualize some functions and to compare their behaviors graphically.

Part 3

The Traveling Salesperson Problem (TSP for short) is one of those NP-complete problems that seem to take an inordinate amount of time to solve. It is explained on p. 538 of your textbook, but we'll summarize it briefly here.

First, start the TSP applet and click on *Load Example*. This brings up a five-node graph. Click on *Find Path* and a salmon-colored window shows the most efficient (shortest) path for the salesperson to follow when visiting all the cities.

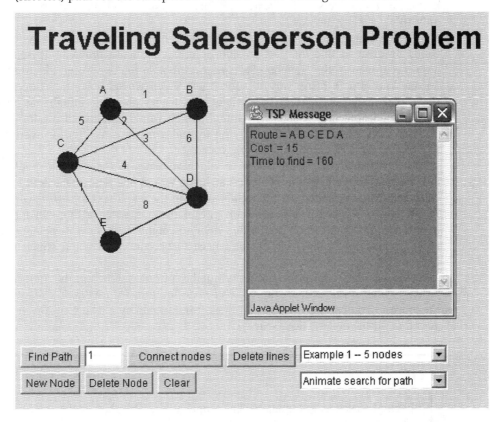

Think of the graph as a map that shows cities A, B, C, D, and E. Some cities have a two-way road between them, with a distance number shown on the road. The distances shown above are not necessarily in scale with the length of the line, but that's okay—graphs are abstract creatures and live by their own rules.

The salesperson must visit all the cities, and wants to save gasoline as well. By starting at city A and going to each city exactly once, ending up back at A, the salesperson can accomplish the first goal, and to some degree the second, since at least he or she will not be backtracking and going through a city more than once. A path that visits all cities exactly once is called a *tour* or a *circuit*.

But wait, the boss has just added a third restriction! There may be several possible tours, but the boss wants the salesperson to use the shortest one. Such a tour is called a *Hamiltonian circuit*, and this is what the TSP applet finds, if there is any possible circuit at all.

When you run the applet, notice the cost measure it calculates. This is the sum of all the numbers (called *weights*) on the lines between the cities. A Hamiltonian circuit has the smallest cost measure of all the circuits (if there are any). Also notice the "Time to find" value, which the applet reports underneath the cost. This is a measure of how many comparisons the program made in order to find the shortest circuit. Notice how it goes up dramatically as you add nodes and try to find a Hamiltonian circuit in a big graph.

While it is easy for us to find all the circuits in the previous graph, and therefore not too taxing to find the Hamiltonian circuit, larger graphs make it harder and harder, both for us and for the computer. While the computer (thankfully) doesn't complain of eye strain or overwork, it *does* take a long time to find the Hamiltonian circuit. By the time we get up to the relatively small number of, say, 40 cities (and, of course, there are many more than 40 cities in the United States, or even in most states), the amount of time the computer needs to find the Hamiltonian circuit is so large that all the protons of the universe will disintegrate first! (Physicists believe that protons will last only 10^{34} years, by the way.)

The fact that it takes so long to solve this problem is really unfortunate, because it would be great to find the best possible solution to such a problem. There are other problems similar to the Traveling Salesperson Problem that we would like to solve, but no one knows of a faster way to solve them. Even worse, no one has been able to prove that no faster solution is possible! This leaves open the tantalizing possibility that an algorithm may someday be found, which would revolutionize a lot of things. But computer scientists have been trying to find a faster algorithm for over 30 years, and they're no closer now than they've ever been.

The TSP applet also allows you to add new nodes to the existing graph. Simply double-click on the empty area and a new node with a one-letter name will appear. To connect it to other nodes, set the weight for it in the small text area (it is currently 1). Then click on *Connect nodes*. Click on one of the nodes and a line will follow your mouse pointer. Click on the destination node to complete the line. Remember the lines represent two-way paths, so you don't need to be concerned about which node you click on first.

You can repeat this process for any number of nodes. Click on the *Stop connecting* button (which is the same as the *Connect nodes* button, with its label changed) to end the process. You can also remove all lines from a node by clicking on *Delete lines*. To get rid of all the nodes, click *Clear*.

Tip

TSP can be used as a standalone Java application. If you use TSP as an application (not as an applet), you can load and save your graphs. To run the Java application, navigate to the folder containing the TSP class files and double-click on the **run_application.bat** file.

Exercise 1

Name _____   Date _____

Section _____

1) Start the "Comparison of several functions" applet and click on the *Example 1* button. The applet runs through a bunch of N values and puts the corresponding f(N) in the text areas. Write down what value N has when the N^N text area first says "too big!" Do the same for the N! and 2^N text areas. You may have to click on *Example 1* several times, watching carefully for when the fields change to "too big!"

2) Type the following function into the first f(N) text space:

   log(log(N))

   (There's no mystical significance to this formula; we're just using it as an example.) Then type in several values of N, one at a time, and press the *Compute* button after each one. Now see if you can get the value 1.0 to appear in the result area by finding a value of N such that log(log(N)) approximately equals 1.0. (Hint: Think BIG! You may not hit 1.0 exactly but you can come close.)

   Take a screenshot when you've found it.

3) Let's experiment with three functions. Click on *Example 3* and three functions will be inserted into the three f(N) text areas.

4) Take a screenshot, print it, and write the order of magnitude in big-O notation next to each of three functions. (See p. 547 of your textbook.)

5) Type 1 into the N text area and press *Compute*. Write down the values of the three functions. Which function gives the biggest answer?

6) Type 3000 into the N text area and press *Compute*. Write down the values of the three functions. Which function now gives the biggest answer?

7) Finally, find a value for N that causes the third function to give the biggest answer.

8) Write down your observations as to the values that these three functions produce for given ranges of N. Is one function always larger than the others? Why or why not?

Exercise 2

Name _____ Date _____

Section _____

1) Start the "Traveling Salesperson Problem" applet.

2) Pull down the examples list and select "Example 1 – 5 nodes."

3) Before the applet finds a path, try to find one yourself. Either list the nodes in order from A back to A, or take a screenshot and highlight the path with a pen.

4) Now click on the "Find Path" button and watch the applet search. Write down the path it found and the cost.

5) Your path might be different from what the applet found. Make a guess as to why the applet found the one it did. (Hint: think of alphabetical order....)

6) Are there only two circuits in this 5-node network?

7) Is the network shown in this 5-node example a directly (fully) connected network? (See Laboratory 15.) To refresh your memory, a directly connected network is one where there is a single wire between any two nodes.

8) Following is a picture of an 8-node directly connected network.

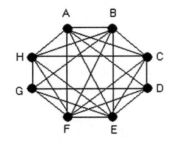

Why is it very easy to find a circuit in a directly connected network?

9) Are there many circuits in a directly connected network? Can you list several others in the 8-node network above?

10) What other network topologies have easy-to-find circuits?

Exercise 3

Name _____ Date _____

Section _____

1) Start the "Traveling Salesperson Problem" applet.

2) Pull down the examples list and select "Example 2 − 12 nodes."

3) Before the applet finds a path, try to find one yourself. Either list the nodes in order from A back to A, or take a screenshot and highlight the path with a pen.

4) Now click on the *Find Path* button and watch the applet search. The applet automatically animates its search by coloring tentative path segments in yellow. Watch the applet run for a few minutes. Did it find a path in that time?

5) Now stop and restart the applet (which you can do by pressing the BACK button on your browser or by closing your browser and beginning over). Select "Example 2 − 12 nodes" and select "Don't animate search." Click on *Find Path*. Write down the path it found and the cost, as well as the time to find it.

6) Did it find the same path that you did? Why did the applet choose the path it did rather than yours?

7) Add one new node and connect it to 3 other nearby nodes. Then click on *Find Path* again and write down the time it took. Was the time about the same as Step 5 above or was it a lot more?

8) Make a guess as to how the time to find increases as you add nodes. (Don't worry about being mathematically precise or figuring out the big-O function.)

Exercise 4

Name _____ Date _____

Section _____

1) Start the "Plotter" applet. Select these functions from the "Choose Function" pull-down menu:

   x^2

   x ln x

   (x^2 is "x squared" or "x multiplied by itself." x ln x is "x multiplied by the logarithm of x.")

2) Which one grows faster? That is, as x gets larger and larger, which function's y value gets larger than the other's? The faster-grower's curve will be above the other one's curve.

3) Take a screenshot and label the two curves, since the Plotter applet doesn't do that for you.

4) Suppose that you heard that Algorithm A's running time function was x^2, meaning that if the problem size is k, then the number of time steps it would take to find the solution is k times k. Suppose that Algorithm B's running time function was x ln x. If both algorithms solve the same problems, such as "sort a list of numbers," which one should you use?

5) Find a function that can be called *linear*, that is, whose plot is a straight line.

6) Why should we try to find algorithms that have linear functions for their running times?

Exercise 5

Name _____ Date _____

Section _____

1) Start the "Plotter" applet. Select these functions from the "Choose Function" pull-down menu:

      x^x

      x^4

2) Take a screenshot and label the two curves.

3) Which function seems to grow faster, based on the picture?

4) Now change the maximum Y axis to be 1000, instead of 8. Take another screenshot.

5) Do you want to change your answer to Question 3 above? Why?

Exercise 6

Name _____ Date _____

Section _____

1) Start the "Plotter" applet. Select these functions from the "Choose Function" pull-down menu:

   1/x

2) What power of x is the same function as 1/x?

3) Suppose that somebody told you that Algorithm C's running time function for positive values of x was 1/x. What would this mean as x increased? That is, as your problem size increased, what happens to the running time of the algorithm?

4) Is this realistic? If not, why not?

Deliverables

....

Turn in your hand-written answers on a sheet of paper, along with the screenshots required for the two exercises.

Deeper Investigation

....

In this lab, we have investigated only one aspect of the limits of computing. The textbook describes this aspect and many others. The term given broadly to this part of computer science is *theoretical computer science*. Some of its findings are quite old, such as Turing's work, dating back to the 1930s, and some are at the cutting edge of the field. In the meantime, several questions remain unanswered.

Let's think about how we might measure software quality and complexity. Think back to some of the algorithms presented in Chapter 9 of the textbook. What kinds of measurements can you come up with that would begin to measure the quality or complexity of a chunk of code? Obviously, the number of lines in the code is a very crude measure. What more clever, insightful methods can you devise?

Turning our attention to the Traveling Salesperson Problem, we mentioned that finding the shortest path through a 40-city grid would probably take more time than the universe has to offer. Computer scientists have attempted to short-circuit this impossible situation by finding paths that may not be the best, but are pretty close to the best. Think of a way that we could change the Traveling Salesperson algorithm to do this. Currently, the algorithm looks at *all* paths and finds *all* circuits. Then it compares them and chooses the circuit with the smallest cost. (Hint: Think of an egg timer!)

Though the Traveling Salesperson Problem may strike you as silly and not terribly important, there certainly are real-world applications that are similar. Can you think of one or two? (Hint: Think about the Internet, think about security, and think about packet routing.)